Using Readers in Language Teaching

by Tricia Hedge

D1447669

Essential Language Teaching Series

General Editors: Roger H Flavell

Monica Vincent

**MACMILLAN
PUBLISHERS**

First published 1985
Reprinted 1987

Published by *Macmillan Publishers Ltd*
London and Basingstoke
Associated Companies and Representatives in Accra,
Auckland, Delhi, Dublin, Gaborone, Hamburg, Harare,
Hong Kong, Kuala Lumpur, Lagos, Manzini, Melbourne,
Mexico City, Nairobi, New York, Singapore, Tokyo

Hedge, Tricia
    Using readers in language teaching. — (Essential
    language teaching series)
    1. English language — Study and teaching —
    Foreign speakers
    I. Title   II Series
    428.6'4'071   PE1128.A2

ISBN 0 – 333 – 33388 – 8

I should like to thank Monica Vincent for her help and advice,
Norman Whitney for his excellent practical tasks and worksheets
and the staff and students of Ealing College of Higher Education
for their ideas and contributions.

Contents

Introduction v

1 Types of control in graded Readers 1
1.1 Lexical control 2
1.2 Structural control 9
1.3 Information control 14
1.4 The process of simplification 16
1.5 Some issues in simplification 20

2 How graded Readers can help the language learner 22
2.1 Developing knowledge of the language 22
2.2 Developing knowledge of language use 26
2.3 Developing reading skills and strategies 31
2.4 Developing attitudes to reading 34

3 Selecting Readers 37
3.1 Motivation and educational factors 38
3.2 Background knowledge 44
3.3 Language level 49
3.4 Technical presentation 56
3.5 A personal questionnaire 59

4 Introducing graded Readers 62
4.1 When to introduce graded Readers 62
4.2 Preparing learners for extensive reading 63
4.3 Integrating Readers and reading activities 75

5 The class library 83

5.1 Organising the library 83

5.2 Keeping a record 88

5.3 Directing and encouraging the choice of books 91

5.4 Practical suggestions for promoting books 92

6 Individualised Reading 94

6.1 Time for reading 94

6.2 Interviews 95

6.3 Preparing for reading 96

6.4 Using cassettes for individualised reading 100

6.5 Individualising activities 101

7 Using a class Reader 109

7.1 Starting a new Reader 109

7.2 Methods of reading the book 112

7.3 Planning a scheme of work for a Reader 116

7.4 Asking questions about books 118

8 Using Readers as an extra classroom resource 120

8.1 Readers as a resource for language study 120

8.2 Readers as a resource for skills work 133

Conclusion 140

Appendix I Readers for Africa 141

Appendix II Publishers' handbooks 142

Appendix III The Malaysian reading scheme 143

Bibliography and further reading 146

Index 149

Acknowledgements 151

Introduction

Michael West, a name much associated with the development of graded Readers, wrote as long ago as 1950,

> Few things are more encouraging to a child who knows some 1,500 words (say) of English than to pick up a book written within that vocabulary and find that he is actually able to read it and enjoy a story which is (at least) an enthralling approximation of the original. (West 1950)

The same is undoubtedly true of adult learners.

However, this encouraging experience is only likely to occur if several factors are operating successfully. First of all, the book must be right for the student. This means, on the one hand, that the subject matter should be motivating because it relates to the student's personal interests or knowledge. On the other hand, it means that the level of language difficulty should be appropriate to the student's competence in English. Both of these conditions need to be met if a particular book is going to be an effective language learning aid to a particular student. Secondly, graded Readers will only be useful if the teacher is able to exploit them fully, selecting activities and using a range of techniques to develop language learning both in and out of the classroom.

On both counts, appropriacy of books and choice of methodology, success depends on the knowledge, sensitivity and professional skills of the teacher. Every teacher needs to be able to make a sensible selection of graded Readers, which means being familiar with what is available and understanding the various criteria used for linguistic grading. And every teacher needs to learn how to design and initiate activities to accompany reading.

This book is intended as a guide to the teacher on the selection and use of graded Readers. It has been written:

- for teachers of English as a foreign language to adults or children
- for teachers of English as a second language in countries where it is the official language of education
- for teachers of English to immigrant groups of adults or children in English-speaking countries.

It sets out to serve both as an introduction to teacher trainees and as a source of ideas for the experienced teacher who wishes to develop new approaches.

The book is essentially practical, though its suggestions for learner activities and teaching procedures develop from a conceptual framework based on current ideas about reading and current methodological approaches in teaching English as a second or foreign language. It begins by describing how the language of graded Readers is controlled and how the nature of that control makes Readers a valuable aid in language learning. Chapters 3,4 and 5 move on to questions of selection and organisation, what the teacher needs to look for when choosing graded Readers and how reading resources can be organised in practical ways. In Chapters 6,7 and 8 the focus is on practical suggestions for reading activities inside and outside the classroom and on the design of supplementary work for students.

Throughout the book the emphasis is on the kind of reading usually known as extensive reading. In a carefully balanced English language course, ideally the learners will experience both intensive and extensive reading. These two types are mutually dependent for the development of fluent reading in English as a foreign language. Through intensive reading activities in the classroom, students are trained in the various skills and strategies necessary for progress in reading. The activities involve a close study of texts and an examination of the features of English at the various levels of word, sentence, paragraph and whole text. Intensive reading activities are designed to help students in the detailed comprehension of shorter texts and in the interpretation of the writer's intention in relation to the students' ideas, knowledge and attitudes. This kind of reading activity has been called 'skills training' (Munby 1979: 143). Another book in this series (Williams 1984) looks at this aspect in detail.

The aim of extensive reading is to give students the opportunity to practise the skills learned through intensive study by reading longer texts and developing the ability to read quickly in English. The ultimate goal is to read authentic texts fluently, for pleasure, information and reference. Even at lower levels of learning, teachers can work towards this goal by using graded or simplified Readers.

One final point needs to be made by way of introduction. In setting out to provide opportunities for extensive reading, each teacher will be working in a different situation with its own possibilities and problems. Here are some examples:

A Heather teaches a group of twenty adult students in an adult education centre in Scandinavia. They attend a part-time class two evenings a week. Heather's students are prepared and able to contribute a small sum of money each, with which she buys fifty different Readers from local ELT agents. After consulting her students, Heather carefully selects books to suit their interests. The books form a class library. One evening a week Heather brings all the books to class in a box and students browse through them and choose the ones they want to borrow to read at home. Heather has access to facilities for making extra materials to accompany the graded Readers.

B Hedi works in North Africa in a secondary school with a class of 35 fifteen year old boys. He is assigned a class set of a simplified English novel for the term. The tradition in the institution where he works is to have a reading class every week. His students are well motivated but their only exposure to English is in Hedi's classroom. He obviously wants to exploit the Reader as fully as possible as an extra learning resource. His only teaching aids are blackboard and chalk.

C Aparna teaches a class of fourteen children between the ages of eleven and thirteen in a Language Centre in Britain. Children attend this unit when they first arrive in Britain and go on to secondary schools when they have learned sufficient English. The Centre has resources to buy materials and Aparna's classroom has a library corner where a selection of graded Readers is on display. Children can choose books from this to read at home, during lessons when they have finished other tasks, or during private reading lessons. Aparna has included among the Readers some which have less structural control and a more natural range of language forms because she feels this will best help her students to deal with the language they hear around them every day.

D Julita teaches a class of eight year old boys and girls in Jamaica. Standard Jamaican English is used in school but many of the children speak a Creole variety of English at home. Julita chooses sets of story books to read with her class. These are designed to help with the special language needs of these children and the subject matter is in keeping with the lives and interests of eight year old West Indian primary children. Many of the stories have been specially written by Caribbean writers.

These few examples show something of the range of teaching and learning situations in the world of English as a foreign or second language. All kinds of factors determine the degree of freedom a teacher has in selecting Readers, the type of Readers which might be selected and the possibilities for developing a flexible approach.

This book will therefore try to tread a middle path, discussing general principles and introducing practical suggestions which are applicable to many situations and adaptable to others. Teachers will be able to select what is most useful to specific educational contexts and particular groups of students.

1 Types of control in graded Readers

A wide range of graded Readers is now available at different levels, levels achieved either by writing a new story to careful language specifications, or by abridging and simplifying an existing book to a required level or grade. For example, *Great People of Our Time* (Carol Christian) is one of the author's own set of biographies specially written to Range six of Macmillan 'Rangers'. 'Heinemann Guided Readers' present a different type of Reader in a retold version of *A Town Like Alice* (Nevil Shute), in which D R Hill takes the original story line and rewrites it in a new framework to the language specifications of the intermediate level of this series. In contrast to both of these, *Hotel* (Norman Wymer) in the 'Longman Simplified English Series', is an abridged and simplified version of Arthur Hailey's novel, which follows the text of the original closely but uses various principles of simplification to bring it to the required language level.

The most logical way to begin a book like this on graded Readers is to look at how they are graded or made 'easy'. What exactly are the principles of linguistic grading used? What do the procedures for simplification involve? Or, to put it another way, what types of control operate on the language of graded Readers?

That is not to say that the linguistic grading system is the only factor which should influence teachers and students in their selection of Readers. Enjoyment and motivation should certainly come first. Given the choice, students usually select books which look interesting. However, any teacher with a professional interest in the reading development of his students will want to know the best ways to contribute to that development by the selection of interesting and useful Readers at appropriate language levels. And this entails understanding something of the technical background of grading and simplification processes.

When publishers produce series of Readers which are graded at progressive levels of difficulty, the editors and writers are working on assumptions about what constitutes difficulty in reading. And this, in turn, involves assumptions about what happens in reading comprehension, how a foreign language learner deduces meaning from text, and what features of a text cause difficulty in the process of inferring meaning. If the purpose of graded Readers is to introduce students gradually to increasing levels of difficulty in text, then each level must achieve a controlled balance between familiar and unfamiliar language. The language of a graded Reader therefore demonstrates one or more types of control. The first and most obvious of these, the grading of vocabulary, can be called lexical control.

1.1 Lexical control

Lexical control is a first principle in graded Readers. A brief look at publishers' catalogues will quickly establish how Readers are carefully graded into levels so that students progress gradually through successive levels with increasing ranges of vocabulary. For example, Longman's 'New Method Supplementary Readers', otherwise known as the 'Squirrels Series', which present classics of English literature in simplified form for 'young learners', range from a vocabulary of about 450 words at Stage 1 to about 2300 words at Stage 6. A series of Readers is usually accompanied by a Teacher's Handbook or Guide which gives the complete vocabulary list and indicates the level at which a lexical item is first introduced.

1.1.1 The development of word lists

The vocabulary lists which form the basis of most series of Readers relate back to work done as early as the 1930s and 40s and later revised and modified. To take two well-known series as examples, in the 'Longman Simplified English Series' the books are abridged and simplified to the level of the 2000 headwords of *A General Service List of English Words* edited by Michael West (1953). Another Longman series, the 'Bridge Series', establishes its vocabulary level by reference to the *General Service List* and to the 3000-7000 range of Thorndike and Lorge's *A Teacher's Handbook of 30000 Words*. (1944)

The General Service List has some 2000 headwords, each accompanied by its inflected forms, for example, '*do*, doing, does, done,' together with a list of common derivatives and compounds. Homonyms, such as 'bank' (of a river) and 'bank' (in which to deposit money) are treated as separate headwords and the list includes not only single words but collocations too, such as 'at once' and 'of course'.

A detailed account of the objectives and methodology of early word counts and how these played a part in the development of graded Readers is given by John Bright and G P McGregor (Bright and McGregor 1970: 14-51).

1.1.2 A comparison of current word lists

It is on the two lists discussed above, that of West and that of Thorndike and Lorge, that most published series of graded Readers ultimately base their vocabulary lists. The system of grades within any one series is individual. For example,

- Oxford University Press in the 'Oxford Guided Readers' use five lists prepared by L A Hill at 500, 750, 1000, 1500 and 2075 headwords.
- Macmillan's 'Ranger' series uses eight ranges of approximately

350 words each, chosen for their 'all-round serviceability'.

- 'Collins English Library' uses six levels at 300, 600, 1000, 1500, 2000 and 2500 headwords.
- 'Heinemann Guided Readers' use yet another system of four grades: Beginner level (600 words), Elementary level (1100 words), Intermediate level (1600 words) and Upper level (2200 words), but the vocabulary used at each level is not based on any existing word count or list. The word levels are given because, as the editors believe, 'teachers are accustomed to using vocabulary counts as an indication of reading level'. They have been arrived at by estimating the number of basic words (ie not special to the story) used across a number of manuscripts, which have been prepared with an

> intuitive, commonsense attitude to the control of vocabulary based on the writer's and editor's experience of what vocabulary students can cope with at a particular level.

These few examples demonstrate clearly the lack of any easy correspondence between one publisher's system and another's. Moreover, even where the levels in two series appear to have a similar number of headwords, those headwords are not necessarily the same, and neither may fit the learner's competence if the main course material is from yet another publisher. All of this makes the teacher's task of selecting Readers a difficult and confusing one. This problem will be taken up and discussed in Chapter 3.

Another point that teachers need to be aware of is the amount of variation that exists within one grade and this, too, differs from one series to another. The editors of the 'Collins English Library' are careful to point out that

> few of even the longest readers use more than 20 items of outside vocabulary . . . there are few linguistic distractors.

This is in keeping with the purpose of the series which is to provide books at the learners' level of competence which allows them to 'read through a text at something like normal reading speed'. The quality of careful restriction here contrasts with the deliberate variation that exists within any one level of 'Heinemann Guided Readers'. In this series the editors have included more difficult books within each level 'in order to avoid putting students into the situation of having to make a big leap every time they want to move up from one level to another' and these books are clearly indicated in the list of titles available.

Most series of graded Readers make a distinction between the basic words of each level and other words which relate to the content of the specific text. For example, in addition to the basic, 'core' vocabulary, Macmillan's 'Rangers' present Range words and Topic words, the former printed in bold type throughout the text (Example 1) and the latter listed for the student at the end of the Reader.

Example 1 In Macmillan 'Rangers', Range words are printed in bold type throughout the text.

Sue Mr James! Where are you? Please answer.
Tim Come in here. There's a man in the **bed**. He's **ill**.
Sue It's him! It's Mr James. There's his radio, Tim.

Tim He's ill. There's a phone. Ask for a doctor, Sue.
Sue (*She speaks into the phone.*) **Hallo**! Is that Dr Jones? Please come to 8 Green Street. Mr James is ill.

Sue Good **morning**, Mr James. How are you now?
Mr James (*He looks up.*) I'm not too bad. **Thank you** very much for your help.
Tim Thank my radio, Mr James!

2

Pilbeam's Circus Diana Webster (Macmillan 'Rangers', Range 1)

Obviously a 3000 word vocabulary is insufficient for the reading of all kinds of texts and it is the Topic words that express the special content. As Rivers and Temperley put it (1978: 206), these words are

> the group of words which at any level of reading ability will draw the interest of the student and provide much of the specific information of the text, but which are too specialised to be among the few thousand most frequent words.

In the Handbook to 'Longman Structural Readers', these words are termed 'Additional words' and it is interesting to note the instructions given to writers about the way in which Additional words should be introduced.

> Where other words are appropriate for the subject matter, they may be introduced as additional vocabulary providing each word is repeated within a few lines or again within a few pages. The first repetition should be in a slightly different type of sentence to the first introduction wherever possible, to help the student deduce the meaning of the word.

In this way the foreign language reader is encouraged to use the techniques of the native speaker when dealing with an unknown word, to make an intelligent stab at the meaning of the word through clues in the context. The familiar basic vocabulary of the sentence provides the learner with a context from which to infer the meaning of the unfamiliar word. This process can be seen at work in Example 2. It is possible to get an idea of how the text would look to a foreign language learner by replacing the new words, those not introduced at Stage 4, with nonsense words.

How easy do you think it is to deduce the meanings of the words from the general context or from clues such as the position of the word in the sentence?

Example 2 How the text might look to a foreign language learner

Chapter 1   My Father's Watch

In our village, there were only six good clocks. The biggest clock was in the church stram where everybody could see it. My father owned one of the others. It stood in our kitchen. He wound it every night before he went to bed.

Once a year, the clockmarret came from Winchester. He came on his horse. He cleaned the clock in the church stram first. Then he cleaned ours, and he set its hands to the correct time.

My mother always gave him something to drink, and they talked together. He told her about his life in Winchester. This was our nearest town. It was very old. Some people say that English kings once lived there, in a jurrip. That was a long time ago; but parts of the jurrip still remain.

My father was a barlim and he was a busy man. When the clock had been cleaned, he always left the room. 'Women can taddle their time with stories,' he said, 'but men have work to do.' And he went back to his barl.

But my father's greatest fastam was not the clock. It was a watch. It was fixed to a wol so that you could wear it on your prad.

My father kept it in a locked dimp in his desk. He only brought it out on special days. Then he fixed the wol round his prad and he wore the watch for a few hours. After that, he locked it in its dimp again.

The White Mountains p1, John Christopher
abridged and simplified by A G Eyre ('Longman
Structural Readers' Stage 4)

The English words which have been replaced are *tower, clockmaker, tower, castle, castle, miller, waste, mill, treasure, strap, wrist, case, strap, wrist, case*. The Additional words in this text are 'tower' 'strap' and 'wrist', which, as instructed, are duly repeated and their meanings can be guessed from the context.

Another much-exploited device in Readers is to use pictures to illustrate meaning and many lower level Readers are of the cartoon picture type with accompanying text. Example 3 shows the density of unfamiliar words and the interdependence of text and illustrations.

How easy do you think it is to guess the meanings of words from clues in the picture?

Example 3 . . . interdependence of text and illustrations . . .

It is the 26th July. Mr and Mrs Davies and Catherine are in the car. They are stribbing to the flamp.

"Catherine, have you got your giltip and your valmet?"

Mr Davies says.

"Yes, Dad," Catherine says. "You've asked me that ten grums. Here's my giltip and here's my valmet."

Have You Got Your Ticket? p4 Ian Serraillier
('Longman Structural Readers' Stage 2)

This extract is also a good example of how a student's background and general experience will help in guessing meanings. It is fairly common knowledge that passports and tickets are needed for a journey by air, but if stories contain culturally unfamiliar situations, pictures can be invaluable aids to comprehension.

A final point worth mentioning before turning to the area of structural control is the relationship between levels in Readers and student competence. This is a complex issue, each series setting out slightly different relationships between its levels of headwords and levels of student competence. Sometimes the relationship is expressed in terms of general labels such as beginner, elementary, intermediate, advanced and so on. Sometimes it relates in a more detailed way to a wider range of teaching materials produced by a particular publisher. It is always worth finding out whether a set of Readers has the same grading system as main course books produced by the publisher. Chapter 3 takes up suggestions for how an individual teacher can select books appropriate to the competence of specific groups of students.

1.2 Structural control

Vocabulary is one factor in the ease or difficulty of reading texts but obviously not the only one. It is quite easy to think of a sentence like 'If they do what he does, then we will not go with them', which consists of short simple words but which is structurally difficult for a language learner. In recent years a good deal of research has been undertaken on readability, or in other words, the linguistic and conceptual difficulty of a text. Most of this research has related to mother tongue readers but the criteria for assessing linguistic difficulty are also appropriate to foreign language learning. Most readability studies take account of word frequency, sentence length and sentence complexity.

Sentence length is used as a grading principle in many graded Readers. The permitted sentence length at the beginner level of 'Heinemann Guided Readers' is 'two clauses forming a compound sentence with the conjunctions *and, but* and *or*'. The writers of 'Longman Structural Readers' are given similar suggested limits of length at Stage 1, but it is difficult to isolate sentence length from sentence complexity as factors in text difficulty.

Reading difficulty caused by sentence complexity can be of different kinds. Colin Harrison (1980:22) makes this point when he writes,

> A passage can be difficult if it is very complex in structure because it puts too great a load on short term memory and information processing capacity. However, it can also be difficult if it is too compressed, and the reader has too few clues to allow him to reconstruct the intended message quickly and correctly.

It is possible to look at the language of a well-known novel and see how these kinds of difficulty present themselves (Example 4).

> Take these two sentences. What kind of difficulty do you think each sentence might present to a learner of English?

Example 4 . . . reading difficulty caused by sentence complexity . . .

Although falling short of the length of Mississippi-Missouri, the Nile is at the head of all rivers as regards the length of its basin, which extends through 35 degrees of latitude.

The Savage had retreated towards cover, and now, in the posture of an animal at bay, stood with his back to the wall of the lighthouse, staring from face to face in speechless horror, like a man out of his senses.

(*Brave New World* Aldous Huxley (1981))

In the first sentence the clause structure is complex and the reader has to remember the information of the subordinate clause at the beginning before reaching the noun 'the Nile' to which it refers. The second sentence contains at least five pieces of information about the position, feelings and actions of the Savage and compresses them into a string of clauses.

Graded Readers deal with the problem of structural or syntactic complexity by using a structural grading scheme, some more rigid than others, but all following an order of structures familiar to language teachers and corresponding to the grading of most structurally based course books.

> Compare the two tables of structures for level 1 of two different series of graded Readers (Figures 1 and 2). What similarities and differences can you find?

Figure 1 Extract of structures at Range 1 from *Guide to 'Rangers'* (Macmillan)

Structures	Examples
1.1 Verb forms	
general	I'm going out tonight.
1.1.1. Affirmatives, and Negatives using *not* (including the short form)	You're not thinking about the story. Jill doesn't work now.
tenses	I'm eating at Michael's house.
1.1.2. Present Continuous (including short forms of the verb *to be*: e.g., *I'm, You're, He's, They're, etc.*)	You are playing a game. He's looking at some pictures.
Also with future intention.	They're not coming on Wednesday.
1.1.3. Present Simple	I understand everything. She's awake but Bill's asleep.
imperative	Write your name here.
1.1.4. Affirmative and Negative, with or without *please*	Please wait for me. Stop! Don't quarrel any more.
interrogative	Is Mr. Smith's car ready?
1.1.5. Of all Range 1 verb forms	Are two of the boys coming? Have all of them got chairs? Can the dog ride with us?
1.1.6. Interrogative words — *what, which, who, when, where, whose, why, how (many)* — both as adjectives and pronouns	Why are you crying? Which pipe is mine? Which is your flat? How many horses are there? Who's going by bus?
auxiliaries and special verb forms	It's coming out of its box.
1.1.7 *can, come out (of), go back* (involving direction), *take away, have (got) to do*: in their literal, concrete meanings only	Go back to bed. Take that boy away. I'm not going to wait for Sally. Joe has got to find his keys.

Verb Phrase elements (VP = be + NP/ADV/ADJ or VERB [+NP] [+ADV]

8 PRESENT SIMPLE	*be; have got* (= 'possess') other VERBS as Basic or Additional Vocabulary
9 PRESENT CONTINUOUS	with present (not future) reference) not *be* or *have*
10 MODALS	*going to* (with future reference) *can* (= ability or permission)

Simple elements and types

11 NEGATIVE STATEMENTS	with *not/n't*, incl *do/does* (statements only: no negative questions or imperatives until Stage 2)
12 *Yes/No* QUESTIONS 1	incl *do/does*; plus short answers
13 *Wh-* QUESTIONS 1	*What* and *Who* only
14 IMPERATIVES	incl eg *Stand up, Please sit down, Look at* NP. *Go there/to* NP, *Come here/to* NP, *please.*

The organisation of items and category headings may differ but the
two tables show the close correspondence at lower levels that one
might expect. Readers produced for a more limited market, for
example West Africa or the Caribbean, may well correspond less to
international series. This is because the structural grading system
can concentrate on the particular, identifiable, learning problems of
local students. For example, the first level of Macmillan's 'Yellow
Bird Readers' for children of 7-13 in the Caribbean focuses on the
correct use of the auxiliary verbs 'to be' and 'to have' as these are
characteristically difficult grammatical points for the learners.

As well as basic structures, Readers introduce other features of written English. The editors of 'Heinemann Guided Readers' give a useful list of some of these:

'Students learning to read have to acquire quickly,

1 the ability to recognize the simple past tense of a number of frequently used verbs since the simple past tense is the tense most commonly used in narration. This is why the simple past tense is used freely in the Beginner Level of the Guided Readers.

2 an understanding of how sentences are arranged in paragraphs.

3 an understanding of the conventions of Direct Speech.

4 an ability to recognize sentence introducers such as 'Then . . .' and 'After that . . .' These sentence introducers are again a feature of written language rather than of spoken language.'

Another possible area of difficulty in a text is found in the reference system, the way in which words such as pronouns substitute for and refer back to noun phrases. Example 5 shows this process at work.

Example 5 . . . the reference system at work . . .

Photographs serve many purposes, and nearly everyone has a camera, but *some photographers* see deeper and show more than others. Like artists and sculptors, *they* are deeply concerned with form, shape and texture as they touch the human spirit. *Such a one* was *Dorothea Lange* who . . .

> *Famous Women of the 20th Century* p19, Carol Christian and Diana Christian (Macmillan 'Rangers' Range 7)

'Some photographers' is replaced by 'they' (a plural form). 'Such a one' (a singular form) is then introduced and also refers back to 'they' and 'some photographers' as well. It also refers forward to 'Dorothea Lange' who becomes the subject of the following text. It would be much simpler for the authors to write something like 'Dorothea Lange was a photographer who was deeply concerned with form, shape, . . .' but at Range 7 of this series it is important to present learners with more complex textual structures. At the lower levels of graded Readers the reference system is carefully simplified. For example, in 'Heinemann Guided Readers' particular attention is paid to the distance between a pronoun and its corresponding noun phrase so that the reader does not lose the thread of who is doing or saying what to whom. See Example 6.

Example 6 . . . the distance between a pronoun and its noun . . .

> **'Mayor Orden is more than a mayor,' Lanser said without listening to Corell. 'The people chose Mayor Orden. He knows what the people are doing. If I watch Mayor Orden, I will know these people, so Orden must stay.'**

> (*The Moon is Down* p16, John Steinbeck retold by M J Paine ('Heinemann Guided Readers' Intermediate))

Notice how many times Orden's name is repeated when it would be more natural to put 'him' or 'he'. The repetition prevents any confusion about who is being referred to.

Of the types of control to be found in graded Readers, structural grading will be the most familiar one to teachers. The concept of information control may not be so familiar.

1.3 Information control

The term 'information control' has been taken from John Milne's Handbook to 'Heinemann Guided Readers'. It is undoubtedly the case that all graded Readers which have been abridged, simplified, or retold from originals are 'controlled' through omission or alteration of descriptive detail, even of events, characters and parts of the dialogue. However, the Heinemann series pays great attention to this type of control in all the Readers and defines it as follows,

> Any book contains within its covers a certain amount of information. This information must be presented to readers in easily digestible amounts if they are to be able to read the story successfully. The writers and rewriters in the HGR Series keep constantly in mind the need to control the amount and flow of information which the reader has to absorb in order to continue reading.

Information control, then, may be achieved through any or all of the following devices.

- Limiting the number of characters or the depth of their definition.
- Controlling the range and complexity of situational or cultural background which may involve omitting episodes of a story.
- Avoiding the technique of flashback in a story and, instead, using a straight, chronological narrative.
- Keeping a careful balance in the length of chapters so that information is presented in 'digestible' amounts.
- Writing an introduction to a story which clarifies context and characters. For example, in Glyn Frewer's *The Raid* (Heinemann) the story opens with careful descriptions of the main characters. Peter Hodson's retelling of *A River Ran Out Of Eden* by James Vance Marshall, makes use of an introduction to the setting of the story in the Aleutian Islands off the coast of Alaska and, with useful illustrations, makes the background clear at once.

It can be seen then that some series of graded Readers involve a variety of controls, working to quite complex specifications which combine criteria for lexical, structural and information control. We can see how these various types of control combine in the process of simplification by comparing an original with its abridged and simplified version and noting what effect this has on the nature and quality of the text.

1.4 The process of simplification

Only a brief comparison is possible within the confines of a book like this but it should serve to illustrate some of the points made earlier about the techniques of grading and simplification.

> Look at the two versions of a passage from 'Brave New World' in Examples 7 and 8. What differences can you find in the lexis used, the structure of the sentences and the information included?

Example 7

The Park Lane Hospital for the Dying was a sixty-storey tower of primrose tiles. As the Savage stepped out of his taxicopter a convoy of gaily-coloured aerial hearses rose whirring from the roof and darted away across the Park, westwards, bound for the Slough Crematorium. At the lift gates the presiding porter gave him the information he required, and he dropped down to Ward 81 (a Galloping Senility ward, the porter explained) on the seventeenth floor.

It was a large room bright with sunshine and yellow paint, and containing twenty beds, all occupied. Linda was dying in company — in company and with all the modern conveniences. The air was continuously alive with gay synthetic melodies. At the foot of every bed, confronting its moribund occupant, was a television box. Television was left on, a running tap, from morning till night. Every quarter of an hour the prevailing perfume of the room was automatically changed. 'We try,' explained the nurse, who had taken charge of the Savage at the door, 'we try to create a thoroughly pleasant atmosphere here — something between a first-class hotel and a feely-palace, if you take my meaning.'

'Where is she?' asked the Savage, ignoring these polite explanations.

The nurse was offended. 'You *are* in a hurry,' she said.

'Is there any hope?' he asked.

'You mean, of her not dying?' (He nodded.) 'No, of course there isn't. When somebody's sent here, there's no . . .' Startled by the expression of distress on his pale face, she suddenly broke off. 'Why, whatever is the matter?' she asked. She was not accustomed to this kind of thing in visitors. (Not that there were many visitors anyhow: or any reason why there should be many visitors.) 'You're not feeling ill, are you?'

He shook his head. 'She's my mother,' he said in a scarcely audible voice.

Brave New World p160, Aldous Huxley (Granada
Publications Ltd. 1981)

Example 8

The Park Lane Hospital for the Dying was sixty floors high and brightly painted. As the Savage got out of his helicopter several gaily-coloured planes rose from the roof. They flew away across the Park, taking dead bodies to the London Crematorium.

John was directed to Room 81, a large bright room. Here, Linda was dying, together with nineteen other old people. The air was alive with music. At the foot of every bed was a television set. Every quarter of an hour the scent of the room was changed.

'We try,' said the nurse, 'to make things as pleasant as possible.'

'Where is she?' asked the Savage.

The nurse was annoyed. 'You *are* in a hurry,' she said.

'Is there any hope?' he asked.

'You mean of her not dying? No, of course there isn't. When somebody's sent here, there's no—' Noticing his sad face, she stopped. 'Why, what's the matter?' she asked. She was not used to seeing sad visitors. In fact, she was not used to visitors. Very few came. 'You're not feeling ill, are you?'

The Savage shook his head. 'She's my mother,' he said softly.

> *Brave New World* pp56-57, Aldous Huxley,
> simplified by S H Burton ('Longman Structural
> Readers' Stage 6)

In order to make the novel accessible to English language learners at the pre-intermediate level, lexical, structural and information controls have been applied.

1.4.1 *Information control*

In terms of length, the original is 306 words to the simplified version's 191. In fact, what actually happens is that the second version is a kind of summary which gives the main events with sufficient description to add colour and retain a little of the original 'flavour'. The sequence of events and the dialogue remain true to the original. The background setting is altered. Slough becomes London. It seems reasonable enough to simplify the geography which will mean very little to most foreign readers. The character of the 'presiding porter', unnecessary to the plot, is cut out neatly by the passive construction, 'John was directed . . .'. Apart from these, most simplification is achieved by omission of descriptive detail, the 'Galloping Senility Ward', the 'primrose tiles', 'the synthetic melodies', and the nurse's unwittingly ironic comparison of the ward to a cross between 'a first class hotel and a feely palace'. Unfortunately, in losing this detail, the simplified version loses much of the wit and individual style of the author, a general problem with graded Readers and one almost impossible to solve in simplification to this level. Davies and Widdowson (1974:190), epitomise this problem when they write,

'The original *recreates* the incidents, the simplified version simply *reports* them.'

1.4.2 *Lexical control*

Apart from the words omitted in the descriptive detail because they are thought to be too difficult, the following substitutions have been made:

1	2
darted	flew
a sixty storey tower	sixty floors high
in company	together with
perfume	scent
offended	annoyed
startled by	noticing
broke off	stopped
accustomed to	used to

in a scarcely audible voice	**softly**
the expression of distress on	**his sad face**
his pale face	

The last two items involve structural changes as well.

Some of these substitutions are immediately understandable: the replacement of a phrasal verb 'broke off' with a familiar synonym; the easier, more everyday 'used to' instead of 'accustomed to'; a simple adverb 'softly' or noun phrase 'his sad face' to replace more complex phrases.

It is interesting to note that both 'perfume' and 'scent' are new words at Stage 6 and to consider why one has been thought more suitable than the other. In the context of the sentence the word 'perfume' has high information value. In other words, it is not possible to understand the meaning of the sentence unless the meaning of 'perfume' is clear. The information in the rest of the sentence does not help. We could substitute 'light' or 'temperature' for 'perfume'. A student who did not know the meaning of 'perfume' would have to look it up in a dictionary, so why is it preferable for him to learn 'scent' which he would also have to look up? Presumably there is a case for arguing that 'scent' is a more useful word because it is generalisable to more situations than 'perfume'. 'Scent' is in the *General Service List* but 'perfume' is not, though there is a comment that 'perfume' is a useful word to have for this meaning of 'scent'.

In other cases, words which are in fact guessable from context, eg 'startled by' and 'sixty storey tower', have been replaced. Presumably the rationale here is that fluency of reading has been given preference over the hesitation that guessing new meanings might create.

The final sentence of the simplified version demonstrates the earlier point made about the pronoun reference system, where 'he' in the original has been replaced by the full phrase 'the Savage' to avoid any possible confusion.

These examples show some of the devices and decisions used in simplifying vocabulary.

1.4.3 *Structural control*

Modifications to lexis are closely related to structural control, as seen in the reduction of 'the expression of distress on his pale face' to 'his sad face'. The idiomatic form 'if you take my meaning' has been omitted. The second sentence of the original, with its many clauses and heavy information load, has been replaced by two simpler sentences in the simplified version. In one case a structure 1 has been completely replaced by 2.

1	2
Not that there were many visitors anyhow: or any reason why there should be many visitors.	**In fact she was not used to visitors.**

Here the information content has been retained in a simple structure and the repetition of forms in version **2** manages to keep a sense of irony,

> 'She was not used to seeing sad visitors. In fact, she was not used to visitors.'

These few points should serve to demonstrate the processes at work in simplifying syntactic difficulty and how difficult it is to achieve a balance between careful syntactic grading and quality of style.

1.5 Some issues in simplification

It is appropriate at this point to ask a question, one taken from Davies and Widdowson (1974:183)

Does the simplification of linguistic elements necessarily result in the simplification of the text as a piece of communication?

It is a question worth asking because many teachers feel concerned about the effect of simplification, or writing to specific grading principles, on the nature and quality of text presented to language learners. There is clearly a literary argument here where novels and drama are concerned but there is also a pedagogic one. There has been a reaction in recent years against what Widdowson has called

> The kind of contrived language data which is a feature of many textbooks and which is simply cited to demonstrate how the rules of the language system can be manifested in sentences. (1976)

A simplified version of an original novel, however carefully constructed, cannot hope to keep the original individuality of style. Many of an author's intentions, attitudes, and opinions, normally conveyed through subtlety of style will not be communicated. What a simplified or graded Reader can do, and many succeed in doing, is to present a well written story which keeps the interest of learners and motivates them to go on reading. Graded Readers give students the opportunity to develop increasing knowledge of the language and awareness of how language is used in written texts, so that they will eventually be able to read and respond to the stylistic features of unedited texts. A series of graded Readers can provide a bridge to the successful reading of authentic material.

This brings us to the wider issue of the various ways in which graded Readers contribute to the development of reading ability in foreign language learners. It is to this question that the next chapter turns.

Make a similar comparison between a passage from one of these simplified versions and the original.

Airport Arthur Hailey *Shaka Zulu* E A Ritter	} 'Longman Simplified English Series'
The Prince and the Pauper Mark Twain *The Swiss Family Robinson* J R Wyss	} 'Longman Squirrels Series'
Lucky Jim Kingsley Amis *The Kontiki Expedition* Thor Heyerdahl	} 'Longman Bridge Series'

2 How graded Readers can help the language learner

Having looked at the ways in which graded Readers are made 'easy', the next step is to consider how they can help learners develop competence and confidence in reading in a foreign language. Ideally, when teachers decide to introduce graded Readers into the classroom it will be with a clear idea of their usefulness in language learning and the selection of Readers will be undertaken with definite objectives in mind. So, before suggesting criteria for selecting Readers and discussing possible ways of using them effectively in class — issues to which the rest of this book is devoted — it is important to answer the fundamental question, 'Why use graded Readers?'

2.1 Developing knowledge of the language

The answer that springs most readily to mind is that graded Readers can develop students' knowledge of language, at the levels of vocabulary and structure and at the level of textual organisation.

2.1.1 *Vocabulary*

One answer, often quoted, is this (Michael West 1950: 188)

> It [the graded Reader] reviews and fixes the vocabulary already learned, it stretches that vocabulary so the learner is enabled to give a greater width of meaning to the words already learned.

In fact, as Chapter 1 demonstrated, most publishers see the main function of Readers as reinforcing vocabulary in this way. Every student needs to master a progressively expanding vocabulary, both active and passive. The teacher can introduce new words carefully through the context of lessons or course materials but the main way for a student to gain control of an adequate vocabulary is through reading.

It is through extensive reading that a student can best come to understand which words are appropriate in which contexts. This is a point David Wilkins makes when he writes (1972:132)

> Through reading the learner . . . is exposed to the lexical items embedded in natural linguistic contexts, and as a result they begin slowly to have the same meaningfulness for him that they have for the native speaker.

As a student sees words in different textual contexts, he gradually develops a more complete comprehension of their meaning and possible uses. One might well question whether graded Readers, with their systems of control, do provide 'natural' linguistic contexts. It can be argued that a student will only learn all the subtleties of meaning through reading authentic texts. However, graded Readers undoubtedly offer wider exposure to English than the more limited material of a general course book and therefore provide a 'step on the way' to mastery of vocabulary.

2.1.2 Structures

In a similar way, graded Readers consolidate the structures that students are learning. As pointed out in Chapter 1, 'Longman Structural Readers' are graded structurally 'in the same order as the majority of modern courses' so that teachers can suit the level of difficulty of the books to their students without too much trouble.

This is straightforward enough where students are following a structurally graded course book but what happens when the book is functionally based, as are many more recent courses? Although many of these courses do, in fact, maintain the principle of syntactic control by combining a functional presentation with fairly strict structural grading, there is, nevertheless, an accredited argument nowadays for exposing students to much less restriction of structures from the early stages of learning. So, is there an equivalent argument for less restriction of structures in graded Readers at the beginner level?

There are interesting differences here among the various series of Readers. Some graded Readers, at the beginner level, in an effort to avoid certain structures, present learners with unnaturally restricted language. For example, the first levels of 'Longman Structural Readers' and Macmillan 'Rangers' present narrative entirely in the present simple and continuous forms. This can be confusing to learners in English-speaking environments who are exposed to authentic English outside the classroom where the past tense is normally used for narrative purposes. For all learners, in fact, there is a risk of over-learning a structure like the present continuous and using it inappropriately as a result of seeing it in unrealistic contexts.

To be fair, both of the series mentioned above get around the problem in many Readers by using dramatic script or cartoon form where the limitation to present tenses is a conventional feature of written 'speech'. Similarly, in non-fiction Readers, the use of present tenses to give information, to describe and explain, is clearly appropriate. However, in the case of prose fiction a teacher must decide whether to introduce Readers which oversimplify structure in a potentially confusing way for the sake of giving students extensive reading experience, or whether to delay extensive reading until students have mastered a fair range of structures. If the second alternative is chosen, students can be introduced to Readers such as at the first levels of 'Collins English Library' or 'Heinemann

Guided Readers' which use past, future and present tenses from the beginning.

2.1.3 *Text*

Of course, vocabulary and structure are not the only levels of language that students need to learn and practise. Traditionally, course writers and language teachers have concentrated on practising sentences. Even though these sentences may be presented in short passages and dialogues, the focus has tended to be, not so much on how sentences link and combine to form texts, but rather on using a text as a way of presenting the grammatical patterns of sentences.

Sentences combine in many different ways to form paragraphs, and paragraphs follow on from one another in different ways according to whether they are developing, for example, a story, a biography or a technical description. It is important that students have the opportunity to read a wide variety of text types. They will then become familiar with the ways in which language is structured at a level higher than that of the sentence.

For example, through extensive reading, students can gradually build up an understanding of how linking words, or connectives, are used to develop ideas, give examples, express cause and effect, add information, qualify a statement, contrast things and so on. Those students who are weak or who lack confidence in this area are able to practise following the relationships between sentences in a text. Similarly, extensive reading gives students a chance to follow up more intensive classroom work on understanding syntax and to see examples of how devices such as co-ordination and subordination are used to combine ideas.

Study this passage. What might cause difficulty in reading?

But while these easygoing friendships made her happy, her closer
relationships usually made her miserable. After a year of marriage to
her first husband, Jimmy Monroe, she discovered that he took the
deadly drug, heroin, and could not stop taking it. In trying to understand his need, Billie began taking heroin herself and was never able
to lose the habit even though, at one time, she was put in prison for
it.

> *Famous Women of the 20th Century* p 62, Carol and
> Diana Christian (Macmillan 'Rangers' Range 7)

A Reader at this level can present students with well-developed
paragraphs which demonstrate more complex language devices. It
is not only vocabulary and sentence structure that are important here
for understanding but also the use of the connectives 'but while' and
'even though' and the way in which they signify how one sentence
or part of a sentence relates to another. As students read, these
connectives help them to anticipate the kind of proposition coming
next, a process which is part of fluent and confident reading.

Building up an understanding, through varied reading, of how
connectives like these provide clues to meaning in texts will help
students to develop a deeper comprehension of how meaning is
expressed, and can be grasped. It will help them to follow ideas
through the organisation of information. Another book in this series
(Williams 1984 Chapter 5) provides a detailed discussion of text
structure and reading difficulty.

2.2 Developing knowledge of language use

Another useful function of Readers is that they help the students
to see how the grammar and vocabulary they have learned actually

work in communication; that is, how words and structures are used by writers to express ideas, opinions, and information. A story or a description or a factual account is not just a set of sentences which demonstrate the rules of grammar and a range of vocabulary. It shows how language is used to communicate facts and feelings. In relation to this, it is important to stress that written communication is very different from spoken communication. Obviously speech and writing use the same basic structures and vocabulary, but writers, who do not have face to face contact with their readers, have to use all sorts of linguistic devices to make their meaning clear, to communicate the message they want readers to understand. For example, this writer cannot use stress and intonation to emphasise the point she is making, so she uses a separate sentence.

Example 10 . . . a separate sentence for emphasis . . .

Advertisers show ordinary life as family life, with a family of father, mother and two children. This is the ideal.

Your Choice p 50, Alma Williams ('Longman Structural Readers' Stage 5)

In this way 'ideal' is focused for the reader, because it comes last in its own sentence, but the foreign learner whose first language does not use this kind of device for emphasis has to appreciate how 'this' refers back to the idea in the previous sentence.

Foreign learners who are literate in their first language understand that these differences exist between spoken and written English from their experience of their mother tongue, but they need to learn what devices written English uses to communicate intentions and meanings they are familiar with in their own language. In intensive reading activities, the teacher can point out differences and teach devices, but through extensive reading students can gradually become familiar, as they move to higher grades, with how the devices of written English are used in different contexts.

Graded Readers can also provide some experience of how language is used in spoken communication, although only in a limited way, without the phonological features that mark emotion and attitude. Many students are learning in situations where English is seldom heard outside the classroom and where the only demonstration of spoken forms is by a non-native teacher, whose own knowledge of how English is actually used by native speakers may be limited.

Examples 11, 12 and 13 show fairly natural speech with contracted forms such as 'can't' and 'won't', tag endings such as 'have you?' and 'can you?', slang expressions such as 'OK' and 'copper' and introductory phrases such as 'Well . . .' and 'As a matter of fact . . .'

In some situations, English may only be practised through dialogues and drills in the course book, and these can be unreliable as examples of realistic English. They often practise structures without contextualising them carefully in a functional framework. For example, in the structural course book, 'going to' is traditionally presented as a kind of future tense, probably contrasted with 'will' and demonstrated in one or two situations such as making holiday plans. Graded Readers can extend the contexts and develop the uses of 'going to' by showing speakers expressing different functions.

Examples 11-13 . . . examples of fairly natural speech . . .

Example 11

Bob was out of the water fast.
"Sorry, Dad," he said. "I was hot."
"Take a good look into the water," said his father. "Can you see him? No? OK, you can take a drink. But don't go into the river.

Crocodile p14, K Cripwell ('Collins English Library' Level 1)

Example 12

Izard was looking uncomfortable. Twice he opened his mouth to speak, and shut it again. At last he said, 'Pengilly, I'm sorry, but we can't help you any more. We can't watch West. The managing director won't allow it.'

'You've changed your minds, have you?' said Pengilly, with surprise. 'Well, now you know what S means.'

'Do I? What does it mean?'

Mogul p18, John Elliot ('Longman Structural
Readers' Stage 5)

Example 13

' I know, Roy. I know,' said Maureen. ' I was only joking. But you can't really blame me if I worry about you, can you? As a matter of fact . . .'

' Yes? ' asked Roy. ' What's up now? '

' Well,' said Maureen. ' My mum said I wasn't to tell you this, but I said I was going to anyway. You know that *copper* – Detective Sergeant Veeder? '

Grandma George in the Underworld p22, Ron
Deadman (Macmillan 'Rangers' Range 6)

Study Examples 14, 15, 16 and 17 and describe the different functions of 'going to'. You should be able to find these:
- stating an intention   ● giving information
- making a promise   ● insisting
- protesting

Example 14

> He was caught up in the crowd of
> soldiers and carried on so fast that his
> feet hardly touched the ground.
> Suddenly he recognised the
> Lieutenant. 'Aren't we going to fight?'
> he cried.

> *Johnny Ring* p23, Carol Christian (Macmillan
> 'Rangers' Range 4)

Example 15

Within ten minutes the whole village knew about it.

'Old Griffiths is going up to the dam to save us all from
drowning,' joked one.

'The Reverend is going to stop the dam from bursting,'
said another.

> *A Crack in the Dam* p19, Michael Evans
> (Macmillan 'Rangers' Range 6)

Example 16

'But, Max,' said Angela. 'All our friends live
here. And the children go to school here. And
our flat is lovely now.'

Max became angry. 'We are going to move,
Angela. We are going to move next week.'

> *The Sky's the Limit* p11, Norman Whitney
> ('Heinemann Guided Readers' B8)

Example 17

"Dave and I have been naughty boys, that's a fact. But, believe it or not, we're going to be honest members of society when we get out."

"I'm going to find a quiet little place in South America, see? Somewhere thousands of miles from London, anyway. You and your Grandma will go first. By plane, I suppose. Dave and I will join you later."

Grandma George in the Underworld pp41 and 44,
Ron Deadman (Macmillan 'Rangers' Range 6)

In all of these extracts 'going to' expresses futurity but the contexts and functions differ.

Through their reading, students will not only have the structures they have learned in class reinforced, but they will also begin to appreciate the different functions expressed by a structure like 'going to' and will experience the structures in a variety of contexts. In this way they will gain a growing understanding of language use as well as language structure.

2.3 Developing reading skills and strategies

In order to see how graded Readers can best fit into a language learning programme, we need to look in a little more detail at what reading involves for the foreign learner. The problem here is that no-one can give an exact description of what reading is or of how anybody learns to do it. However, research into mother tongue reading has provided useful insights into the reading process in general and many of those insights are considered relevant to foreign and second language teaching.

It is now generally accepted that reading is not the careful recognition and comprehension of each word on the page in sequence. A good reader uses a minimum of 'clues' from the text to reconstruct the writer's message. It is not difficult for a fluent reader to read a text with missing, misspelt or blurred words. Experiments have shown that sometimes readers are not even aware of these things. Their successful reading depends upon their ability to predict what comes next. We read, in a sense, what we expect to read, using our knowledge of language and our knowledge of the topic to predict to a large degree what comes next and so move on quickly. Foreign language learners may have problems in this area. Knowledge of the language may well be inadequate and if the subject is unfamiliar, reading with understanding may be very difficult.

Fluent readers possess many different skills which they apply actively to the reading of a text.

- They predict from syntactic and semantic clues and from their existing knowledge of a subject in the way just described.
- They read in phrases, not in single words and actually skip over words if these are not needed for general understanding.
- They learn to read 'between the lines' and work on the meaning of the text at different levels, understanding information, making inferences and critically evaluating ideas.
- They guess the meaning of new words from contextual clues or by applying knowledge of how words can be formed from others.
- They distinguish fact from opinion and statement from example.
- They follow meaning through a paragraph by recognising signals like 'however' and 'on the other hand' and by understanding how words and phrases like 'it', 'this', 'the latter' and 'these matters' refer back to something earlier in the text.

And this list of 'skills' is by no means exhaustive. Successful reading depends on the interaction of reading 'strategies' for 'processing' the text, background knowledge and linguistic competence.

Many foreign language learners are already readers in one or more other languages and can apply all these skills to reading but often they seem to have difficulties in reading fluently in English, even after building up what may seem to the teacher to be a reasonable knowledge of the language. They become anxious and revert to plodding through a text word by word. The teacher's task is to help students to transfer reading ability from one language to another by encouraging good strategies for successful reading. In other cases the teacher may be dealing with children, or even adults, who are illiterate in their first language. English is the first language in which they learn to read. In either case the key to fluent reading is confidence and, in order to build up confidence, the reading component of an English course would ideally include the following elements of intensive practice:

A *Vocabulary Building*

- learning new words
- developing the student's ability to guess the meaning of words by showing them how structural and semantic clues can help them
- understanding how words are derived by *affixation, compounding* etc.

B *Different types of comprehension work*

- identifying the main points of a paragraph
- following the ways in which meaning links across sentences
- working with cross cultural information about the topics of texts and the assumptions of writers so that students can extract cultural meaning from texts.

The last point is especially important where the cultural distance between the learners and the content of the book is considerable.

However, these kinds of intensive practice are not sufficient in themselves to ensure the development of successful readers. They can activate the transfer of reading skills and strategies from the mother tongue to English, they can teach specific skills like the efficient use of the dictionary, if it is needed, and they can increase the students' general understanding of language and their ability to understand socio-cultural meaning. But of equal importance is the kind of practice that comes from extensive reading, lots of practice in reading different types of material. Only then are students given the opportunity to operate strategies like prediction or guessing word meaning and to develop the ability to follow lines of argument. Intensive reading practice in class needs to be complemented by extensive reading in or out of class.

This is where graded Readers are invaluable. If extensive reading is to serve a useful purpose in terms of developing reading skills, then we can see that there are implications for the type of material which should be made available to students. For example, if students are to develop strategies for guessing word meaning from context, then texts need to present new and unfamiliar words or new meanings of known words, but they should not be so difficult as to undermine the students' confidence by defeating all attempts to understand. Graded Readers, then, present the possibility of controlling the level of difficulty and giving a balance between a challenging and a frustrating reading task.

Similarly, the most effective way of dealing with the problem of cultural meaning in texts is to encourage students to read by themselves, choosing subjects related initially to their own interests so that they bring motivation and experience to reading. As their understanding of other cultures and of unfamiliar views increases through reading, they will bring to their reading activities a gradually increasing capacity to understand the full meaning of texts.

The kinds of opportunities that graded Readers give to elementary and intermediate students before they have the competence to read authentic materials with self-confidence, makes them an invaluable resource for the language teacher. Readers provide an experience for the language learner which builds confidence and encourages independence in reading.

2.4 Developing attitudes to reading

There is a final point worth making before moving on to consider how to choose Readers for a class, and that is the role of reading, and therefore of Readers, in the general education of foreign language learners. This applies particularly in the case of children in school and even more particularly in the case of children who are learning English as a second language. Teachers are educators as well as subject specialists and therefore have a measure of responsibility for the development of the whole child, not just his or her language skills. This is just as true for teachers of English as a foreign language in the school curriculum. Foreign-language teachers often feel that their subject is different and rather isolated from the rest of the curriculum, but in fact they are contributing to a child's development in school in ways they may not even realise.

Part of that development is learning about the role and value of books in learning and in life. We read books mainly for information or for pleasure. One desirable goal of education is training children how to use books to get information. For many children, these reading and reference skills will assume importance later in life when they may well study in higher education and use books published in English to follow their own special subject.

There are many graded Readers now published dealing with specialist and technical topics on engineering, sociology, medicine, and so on, which can be used, along with more general factual books, to familiarise students with factual or 'technical' language. Motivating projects can be devised around them. Teachers can train students to look things up, locate useful information and use it for a realistic purpose. For example, students can be asked to give a very simple short talk or write an account — challenging but worthwhile tasks for intermediate students. In this way Readers can contribute to general curricular objectives and activities within the school and develop the kind of study skills in English that some students will need later.

Reading for pleasure is the other main reason for reading, and here a particular point can be made about using Readers with children. Introducing children to Readers is part of the process of getting children to read of their own accord, establishing reading habits, encouraging them to discover their own tastes and interests, helping them to read critically and think creatively about what they have read. Teachers who introduce Readers into the language learning programme sometimes forget that, while their own interest is in developing the child's knowledge of a foreign or second language and reading skills in that language, the child responds to the content of the book. A sensitive teacher can guide students to absorbing books which motivate further reading. The content of reading, ideally chosen to provide enjoyment and interest, is inseparable from the development of good reading skills.

David Holbrook (1961:159) takes this argument further and makes a point about reading in the mother tongue which applies equally to foreign language readers. He writes:

> Reading a story book has the advantage of giving us the experience of sharing an experience, which we can talk a good deal about. A novel deals at length and in complexity with manners, morals, activities of human beings in different conditions and in different stages of life.

and he goes on to point out that if we give a child boring Readers we make it less possible for the child to develop sensibility and we may 'damage its capacity for living as well as learning to use words.'

If foreign-language teachers are introducing stories, a very common type of Reader, to children, they take on the responsibility for creating a positive attitude towards fiction, a pleasure in reading, enjoyment in imaginative experience. If teachers accept this responsibility, the implications for the selection of Readers are considerable and it is to this process that the next Chapter turns.

3 Selecting Readers

A teacher about to select graded Readers for a class will be concerned with these questions:

What sort of books will be attractive and interesting to my students and encourage them to read?

Which books are appropriate for my students in terms of content and level of difficulty?

The answers to the questions will involve a number of variables. An initial consideration must be how Readers are actually going to be used in the classroom. Many teachers nowadays are concerned to provide class time for individual reading, periods when students can engage in reading as a private activity, selecting books on the basis of their own interests and preferences and reading at their own pace. In these circumstances a varied supply of books will be needed. However, it is also true that the shared experience of class reading, where teacher and class follow a Reader together, is seen as valuable by many educational institutions. The selection of a class Reader, if the teacher is free to choose, will be a compromise decision, taking into account the different ages, sexes, interests and linguistic abilities of the students.

In both of these situations, private individualised reading or reading a book together with the class, a similar set of factors will be important, some relating to the student and some relating to the book. Successful reading is determined on the one hand by the students' abilities, knowledge and interest and on the other hand by the language, content and presentation of the reading book. And all of these factors interrelate. For example, a student who already knows about cars and their workings will easily understand *Your Car and How It Works* (M T Murphy 'Longman Structural Readers'

Grade 4), because he already has the concepts for vocabulary items such as 'differential pinion' and 'distributor cap', and can recognise the labels.

There are four major variables affecting the successful use of graded Readers which teachers need to take into account when making a selection. The first and foremost is the students' motivation. Most people now agree that it is a hopeless and frustrating task to force students to read a book they simply are not interested in. Secondly there is the question of the students' background knowledge and the relationship between the conceptual difficulty of a book and their ease of comprehension. Background knowledge is a general term which may cover cultural knowledge, general knowledge of the world or knowledge specific to the subject matter of a particular book. Thirdly, the language level of a book will be important. And fourthly, it would be a mistake to under-estimate the effect that technical details in the presentation of a book — the use of illustrations, the size of print, the lay-out of the text, the attractiveness of the cover — will have on student motivation and ease of reading.

3.1 Motivation and educational factors

Motivation deserves a good deal of attention as a factor in successful reading development.

3.1.1 Exploiting student interests

Many teachers of English have experienced the situation where a student's interest in the content of a book enables him to overcome difficulties in the language in a way the teacher would not have thought possible. In fact, a reader's understanding varies with the extent to which he is involved with the text. A student who finds the subject matter of a book compelling is much more likely to work his way through a difficult text simply because he wants to know what it says. So it would be a mistake to think that a student should always be discouraged from picking up books which are written at a language level above his supposed competence. On the contrary, the challenge may be immensely rewarding as the student finds himself dealing, relatively successfully, with a difficult text on a subject he is interested in.

Ideally then, the choice of books which are interesting should come first because, however carefully graded the language level, a book will not stimulate students to read if the subject matter does not involve them.

Where group reading is the accepted norm, a sensitive teacher needs to consider the interests and preferences of the class when selecting a Reader. The ideal situation is that of students together deciding on a book they want to read with advice and recommendations from their teacher. Unfortunately this is open to only a small percentage of EFL teachers who work in situations where resources are easily available, usually with adults in the private sector of education systems.

3.1.2 *Considering student needs*

There is another issue facing many teachers in relation to student tastes and preferences and the selection of graded Readers. It can be called the language versus literature question. Should reading books in language classes be the classics of English literature, even at the lower levels of language learning, in abridged or simplified versions such as those in Macmillan's 'Stories to Remember' series (simplified) and the 'Macmillan Student Series' (abridged)? This issue is of especial concern in countries where secondary school teachers of English are often teachers of the mother tongue too. They see their educational role in a wider sense as introducing students to literature and developing good reading habits. Teachers of English as a second language, particularly to children, are under the same kind of pressure. They are familiar with the sort of arguments that place responsibility on them for developing children's love of good literature, their imaginative insights, their capacity for empathy with people, even for developing moral character.

The problem here is that if these arguments are carried over to using Readers in language classes and teachers prescribe what 'good literature' should be read, without taking into account the preferences of teenage students, they may well create a situation where students neither develop an abiding interest in the English literary heritage nor learn to read the English language fluently and with pleasure.

It is also worth remembering that abridgement and simplification of novels is a technique demanding skill and considerable literary sensitivity. In Chapter 1 the comparison of the two versions of a passage from *Brave New World* shows this clearly. It is often difficult to retain the quality and impact of the original. Any teacher wondering whether to choose an abridged or simplified version of a well-known novel would be well-advised to read it carefully and assess how real the characters are, how compelling the theme is, and whether it sustains interest. As West puts it (1967:192)

> Simplification and abridgement have brought to life not a few books which for a foreign reader . . . would otherwise be completely dead: they have also murdered not a few whose lives might have been saved.

If the purposes of using graded Readers are mainly linguistic — extending vocabulary, improving reading fluency — these purposes are much more likely to be achieved if students are able to read books appropriate to their immediate interests and reading preferences in their mother tongue.

Of course these interests will be as numerous and varied as the students themselves but if a teacher is selecting a book for a teenage class and the selection does not have to relate to a study of English literature, there will probably be a far greater chance of initial success if watered-down versions of Thomas Hardy and Charles Dickens are avoided, and if, instead, modern books written in contemporary language are chosen — detective stories, romances, thrillers, factual 'special interest' books as in the Longman 'Galaxies' series — or easily accessible historical fiction like *Outcast* by Rosemary Sutcliffe, adapted by David Fickling for OUP's 'Alpha Historical Fiction'.

3.1.3 *Choosing a variety of Readers*

There is a wide range of Readers available nowadays, books which present themes, stories and subjects that students are likely to want to read about. A class library can be chosen initially with a view to

Figure 3 Dimensions of variety

Different types of book		Different cultural backgrounds	Different types of presentation
Fiction	Non fiction		
Mystery	Biography	Local	Cartoon
Thriller	Travel	British	Pictures with text
Romance	Historical	American	Illustrated prose
Adventure	Discovery	Subcultures	Text with diagrams
. . . .	& invention	in Britain	. . . .
. . . .	. . . .	eg rural	. . . .
. . . .	. . . .	city life	. . . .
. . . .	. . . .	working	. . . .
		class	
		. . . .	
		. . . .	

variety. Then, as teachers get to know their students and their interests and preferences, the library can be modified to include more of the kinds of books that prove popular.

There are several dimensions of variety which a teacher needs to think about. Figure 3 can serve as a checklist to which teachers can add items they feel to be important for their own students.

Figure 4 is a list of forty books selected for a class after talking to the students a little about their tastes in reading. The class was one of twenty adult intermediate students, mostly women, aged 18-40, who attended a part-time English class four mornings a week in Britain. Most were short-stay visitors to Britain, though a few had settled in Britain with their families, so for them English was becoming a second language. The borrowing system was organised through a card index (for details see Chapter 5) and this gave evidence of the most popular books over a four month period. The top ten books have been starred.

The list contains three books (marked with a circle) which are not strictly graded Readers but which proved popular with students, quite possibly because they were a challenge. They are books written for upper secondary school pupils in Britain and, as such, the language is not simplified but is undoubtedly simpler than adult reading material. The stories in these particular books are just as appealing to adults as to teenagers.

It is worth pointing out that there are now many series of Readers produced for English schools which are a useful source of lively, motivating Readers for young and adult EFL students at all levels of competence. Teachers with time and opportunity to browse will certainly find good reading material in series such as Heinemann 'New Windmill Series', Longman 'Imprints', Puffin Books, Macmillan 'M Books' and 'Topliners', Peacock Books, Fontana 'Lions', Methuen 'Magnets', Longman 'Knockouts', Hutchinson 'Spirals', Scholastic 'Hippos', Granada 'Dragons' and Edward Arnold 'Headlines'.

News magazines can also be kept in the class library. An increasing

Figure 4 The contents of a class library

Non-Fiction	*	A Woman's Place?	'Longman Structural Readers' Stage 4
		Your Choice	'Longman Structural Readers' Stage 5
		The Pop Industry	'Cassell Graded Readers' Level 5
		A Taste of Britain	'Longman Structural Readers' Stage 4
		Women in Britain	'Evans Graded Reading' Grade 4
		The Wild West	'Evans Graded Reading' Grade 4
		The Common Market	'Cassell Graded Readers' Level 4
Poetry		The Sun Goes Free	'Longman Structural Readers' Stage 5
Human Interest	*	Upstairs, Downstairs	'Alpha Books' OUP Intermediate
	○	Roll of Thunder, Hear my Cry	'Puffin'
	○	Short Stories from India, Pakistan and Bangladesh	Harrap
	*	A Town Like Alice	'Heinemann Guided Readers' Intermediate
		A Crack in the Dam	Macmillan 'Rangers' Range 6
Science Fiction		Rendezvous with Rama	'Alpha' Science Fiction OUP
	*	Brave New World	'Longman Structural Readers' Stage 6
		Me, Myself and I	'Longman Structural Readers' Stage 4
Romance	*	Love Story	'Alpha Books' OUP Intermediate
		I Know My Love	'Collins Graded Readers' Level 5
		The Valentine Generation	'Longman Structural Readers' Stage 5
	*	Jodie	Nelson 'Getaways'
	*	A Summer Romance	'Longman Simplified English Series'
Modern Classics		Goodbye to Berlin	'Alpha Books' OUP Intermediate
		Animal Farm	'Bridge Series': Longman
		British and American Short Stories	'Longman Simplified English Series'
		Sons and Lovers	'Longman Simplified English Series'

Crime and Selection *	Quiet as a Nun A Scandal in Bohemia Death at the Wedding Rat Race	'Alpha' Crime OUP 'Longman Structural Readers' Stage 4 Nelson 'Streamline Books' Nelson 'Getaways'

Thrillers
 	
    *
 	
    °
	The Lady Vanishes
	The Rose of Tibet
	My Cousin Rachel
	
	After the First
	Death
		'Alpha' Thriller OUP
		'Alpha' Thriller OUP
		'Heinemann Guided Readers'
		Intermediate
		
		Fontana 'Lions'

Stories from Other Cultures *	Stories from the Arab World Princess Moonlight The African Child	'Longman Structural Readers' Stage 4 Macmillan 'Rangers' Range 5 'Collins English Library' Level 4
Biographies	Desiree, Queen of Sweden More People of our Time	'Longman Structural Readers' Stage 5 Macmillan 'Rangers' Range 6
Historical Fiction	The Outcast	'Alpha' Historical Fiction OUP

number of these are now available. Many of the articles and interviews in Penguin's 'Password Series' and those in 'Faces and Places' and 'News and Views' (Berry Newsmagazines) were popular with the class above.

3.2 Background knowledge

Providing motivating content is a prime factor to be considered in selecting graded Readers. So too is the conceptual difficulty of a book. Successful reading in a foreign language, just as in the mother tongue, is affected by the way in which the subject matter of a book relates to a learner's existing background knowledge. And this knowledge is of several kinds.

3.2.1 General knowledge

The first kind can be called general knowledge or understanding of the world and how it works. When teaching children, it is especially important to remember that their 'horizons' are gradually expanding, their understanding slowly developing. Readers can assist this process in valuable ways by giving a sensible mix of the familiar and unfamiliar, and by presenting new things in easily accessible ways. A good example of this is Cassell's 'Spotlight' series of Readers. These take an introductory approach to non-fiction topics and are well presented, entertaining and simple without being patronising. Many of the topics *A Doctor's Day, British Food, The Common Market, Fleet Street, British Industry,* and *The Pop Industry* must present readers with alien background settings and unfamiliar concepts, but the subject-specific vocabulary is 'carefully explained through text, illustration or glossary'. This introductory approach is ideal for learners who know little of these subjects in their mother tongue.

3.2.2 Subject-specific knowledge

Another kind of knowledge which is important for successful reading can be called subject-specific knowledge. Everyone is aware how difficult it is to read a book in one's mother tongue on a new subject where there is new information to assimilate and new terminology to learn. A foreign learner of English is considerably assisted in reading if some of the information is already understood. By beginning with known material a learner is able to use his background knowledge of a particular subject to help with the learning of new vocabulary and the understanding of structure.

Having made this point, it is important to mention the other side of the argument. People learn new things through reading. There is no value in only giving students non-fiction Readers on subjects they already know about without trying to widen their horizons. Part of motivation is reading about interesting new things. In addition to this, it is through reading that students gradually build up the understanding and background knowledge which allow them to read with greater comprehension in the future. This, in fact, is the essence of educational experience of which English as a foreign or second language is a part. Certainly in the secondary school curriculum, reading in EFL lessons can contribute a good deal to educational development.

Many series of graded Readers assist conceptual understanding through various devices such as pictures, diagrams, or glossaries. Many of the 'Collier-Macmillan English Readers', for example, have 'a section of glossary notes explaining vocabulary and the verb forms, historical persons mentioned in the text and cultural patterns which may be unfamiliar'.

Some of these devices will be discussed in more detail later in this chapter. For any EFL teachers who may be concerned about their own lack of background knowledge, one of the first things to consider in selecting Readers is the need for or usefulness of a glossary to which both teacher and students can refer.

The main responsibility for the teacher is to relate the content of Readers to the interests and knowledge of learners as these two factors can compensate for linguistic difficulty in the text.

3.2.3 *Cultural knowledge*

Yet another kind of knowledge that affects successful reading is cultural knowledge. Rivers and Temperley (1978 : 202) call this 'socio-cultural meaning' and they define it as follows:

. . . meaning which springs from shared experiences, values and attitudes. When this type of meaning is not taken into account, or when students interpret an English text according to their own cultural experiences, distortions and misapprehensions result.

This is not just a question of overt reference to places and institutions or customs. These things can often be explained in a glossary. It is also to do with the cultural associations of words and the assumptions that a writer makes in presenting the cultural context of his story.

To take just one book as an example, *Grandma George in the Underworld* (at Range 6 of Macmillan's 'Rangers') is a lively, amusing Reader, written cleverly with wit and style within the lexical and structural restrictions of the grade. The stylish quality depends to a large extent on cultural allusions. The extracts in Example 18 are taken from the first four pages.

How easy do you think it is for foreign learners to understand the cultural allusions in Example 18?

Example 18 . . . cultural allusions . . .

Pat and Dave were always going somewhere to get a drink, thought Grandma George. And that's why they're in the trouble they're in now,

Susan George: pretty as a picture at fourteen, lovely as a prize rose at fifteen, but at sixteen . . . '.

Roy held up his thumb and smiled at her ' All right, Grandma? ' he said.

It might be difficult for foreign students to appreciate the style or even the story fully without some understanding of British culture, customs, traditions, slang, and the non-verbal accompaniments to language. Moreover, it can be difficult for foreign teachers of English to try to explain things which neither they nor their students have ever experienced.

Where learners are far-removed from any English-speaking culture, whether it is British, American, Australian, etc the teacher is under pressure to make a story meaningful by explaining the background and providing cross-cultural references. As students read more widely and gain understanding of the life, customs and attitudes portrayed in their books, they will be more able to appreciate the full meaning of texts and more able to interpret the writers' attitudes. But when students first begin to use graded Readers, teachers need to be sensitive to the problem of cultural context and choose carefully in the light of their own ability to provide a field of reference.

Alternatively, if at all possible, teachers can start by choosing reading materials which relate to the local culture. More of these are now becoming available. For example there are now a number of African novels simplified to the intermediate level : Camara Laye's *The African Child* ('Collins English Library'); Chinua Achebe's *Things Fall Apart* and Mongo Beti's *Mission to Kala* ('Heinemann Guided Readers'); a collection of short stories *Winds of Change* ('Longman Structural Readers') and various titles in Harrap's 'African Library'. These are welcome additions to the already existing collections of Readers suitable for African schools (see Appendix I). Similarly, there are many Readers now available for the local market in the Far East, the Middle East and the Caribbean.

However, the majority of graded Readers are set in a British or American context and, since this is the case, a sensitive teacher may be concerned to ensure that students get as realistic an impression of the culture as possible. This means a judicious selection of books or, at least, discussion of how far characters and situations are representative or how far they are crude stereotypes.

3.3 Language level

Motivation to read and interest in the subject matter of a book are the strongest factors in successful reading but, when selecting graded Readers, a teacher clearly needs to judge the linguistic level of the books and their appropriacy in relation to the developing language competence of the students.

3.3.1 *Using information from publishers*

The first place to look for information and guidance about levels of difficulty is in the handbooks produced to accompany graded Readers (Appendix II). If a class is using a course book from a publishing company which also produces graded Readers, the publisher's catalogue will usually show which grades of Reader relate to the language level of the course book, and it is relatively simple for a teacher to choose a suitable class Reader or collection of Readers.

Problems arise when choosing from a different publisher or when choosing books from many different sources for a class library. Chapter 1 discussed the lack of any clear correspondence between one publisher's system of grading and another's. In terms of vocabulary, for example, even where the levels in two different series have approximately the same number of headwords it does not follow that the words are the same. Parallels in structural difficulty are a little easier to judge since the handbooks mentioned above also contain lists of structures introduced at each level so it is possible to get a rough idea of correspondence between the levels in different series. A useful reference for teachers here is *Readers for Foreign Learners of English* by C J Brumfit (ETIC Information Guide No 7) which lists 1160 Readers in four phases, the first to suit early learners, the second for intermediate to advanced learners, the third for advanced students and the fourth for very advanced learners who are capable of moving on to authentic literary texts. The lists are organised in terms of headwords and so serve as a useful guide as to the relative equivalence between publishers' systems of grading. They are of great value to schools wishing to order a range of books at the appropriate level.

3.3.2 *Language level in relation to other factors*

It is not so much the intrinsic difficulty of the reading matter that needs to be judged as how well a class of students or individuals within that class can cope with the books. If some kind of reading programme exists within the school or institution, there may well be a system of keeping records, whether this is just a brief comment in the class register or a fuller record on individual student cards. Teachers' notes tend to be a better guide than any kind of test result. However, if the class is new and there are no reading records, the teacher will need to use some simple informal strategies for selecting Readers or find more formal ways of assessing the method of selection. Before looking at either of these methods, formal or informal, there are two important points to be made. The first point is that no linguistic evaluation of a graded Reader, whether by 'rule of thumb' or by more sophisticated techniques, is in itself sufficient. It is worth saying again that, given the choice, students start reading books because they look interesting and continue reading books because they are enjoyable. Brumfit (1979 : 6) makes the point neatly:

> Enjoyment at an imaginative level and interest at an intellectual level do not correlate exactly with any linguistic grading system.

If a teacher relies too heavily on linguistic level in the selection of Readers, without giving proper attention to other factors, there can be several unfortunate results.

- Students may be denied access to books which, because of interest in the topics, might spur them on to overcome problems of comprehension.

- Teachers might develop a generally lower level of expectation of student success than is appropriate.
- Teachers might omit lively and interesting books because they seem to be at too high or low a level. In fact, students who read a lot of books at a slightly lower level than they are capable of are developing fluent reading in English and engaging in a positive language learning experience.
- Teachers might include bland reading materials lacking life and character and unable to create interest, for the sake of their controlled vocabularies and structural patterns.

For the above reasons, any kind of readability formula which concentrates on the factor of linguistic difficulty above other factors, should be regarded as a useful guide rather than a constraint. The results of readability measures should serve to point out possible difficulty and frustration and should be looked at in combination with other things such as information from colleagues about popular books, feedback from students and knowledge of their individual tastes and preferences.

The second point worth making is that extensive reading usually takes place in unsupported conditions, that is without a teacher who can explain what the text means. This is clearly the case when students are borrowing books from a class library to read in class time or at home. It is probably also the case on some occasions when students are dealing with a class Reader and may be asked to read silently in class or read a chapter at home. Common sense and experience suggest that for reading at the unsupported level, texts should be simpler than for reading at the supported level where the teacher can deal with any problems.

3.3.3 *General guidelines*

Bearing the above points in mind, it is possible to draw up a list of general principles about language level.

(a) What a foreign learner needs is a book he can read at more or less normal reading speed without frequent pauses to look up unfamiliar words and structures. These should be present to some extent to encourage the strategy of guessing meaning from context but not so numerous that they distract seriously.

(b) In the early stages of language learning, particularly in situations where silent reading is not encouraged to any extent in the general curriculum, the most important thing is simply to encourage reading and provide pleasurable reading experience. For this reason it is especially important to choose texts which contain relatively little unknown language. It has been suggested that new words should be introduced not more frequently than one new in every fifty running words of the text, (Hill & Dobbyn 1979 : 73) 'otherwise the pupil's pleasure and sense of achievement suffer'. If most structure and vocabulary is familiar, a student is able to relate the meaning of what he reads in a particular stretch of the text to what has just preceded it and is able to hold all of this in his immediate memory. In other words, he is able to transfer the habit of fluent reading from his mother tongue to English rather than plodding through the text trying to comprehend individual words.

(c) It is probably more sensible to underestimate a student's ability than to overestimate it. If a student begins with a book which he finds very easy, the material can easily be upgraded. This is a much better situation than giving him a potentially frustrating book. With weaker students, special care is needed to avoid this discouraging experience.

3.3.4 *Procedures for assessing level*

As teachers gain experience in dealing with Readers, they become more familiar with the range of publishers' levels and are more able to make a general evaluation of a book. Experienced teachers are usually able to judge different levels of Reader by looking at such factors as sentence length and complexity, structural patterns and the general level of vocabulary in relation to main course material. However, a newly trained teacher will not have this experience and even a relatively experienced teacher, when meeting a new class, may not have a clear idea of the reading competence of individual students. We therefore need to devise a simple way of predicting how a particular set of students may react to a particular set of books.

Probably the most useful procedure is that of the cloze test. To be most reliable, cloze procedure is best used on large numbers of students at different levels of ability, but it can be used in a rough and ready way to give the teacher some idea of how well a class can cope with a book or collection of books.

Take the example of a class Reader. Some reading will be done in class at the supported level of learning, with the teacher helping. But the teacher also plans to set reading for homework and wants to know how well students will be able to cope with reading on their own.

Here are some simple instructions for cloze testing (an example is given in Figure 5):

1 Choose three passages at random from the book, each one of between 200-250 words.
2 Type or write out each text again on to a stencil so that you can make copies. Leave three or four sentences complete at the beginning of the text. These help the students to understand the context. Then delete every eighth word in the rest of the passage. Make each blank a standard length. This means that students cannot guess the words from their relative lengths but must use other clues.
3 Make a margin down the side of the paper, where students can write the missing words.

Figure 5 Example of a cloze test.

Complete the blanks with the best words you can think of.

Of all the heroes of old Japan, the most famous was Kintaro. He was the strongest and bravest of all the warriors.

Kintaro was the son of a warrior, ... his father died before he was born. . . . . . lived with his mother, high up in . . . . . forest on the steep slope of a . . . . . . His mother was very proud of her . . . . . strong baby. She called him Kintaro — or . . . . . Golden Boy.

As Kintaro grew up he . . . . . stronger and stronger. By the time he was . . . . . years old he could cut down trees . . . . . quickly as any woodcutter. He often went . . . . . the forest with a large axe, given . . . . . him by his mother, and helped the . . . . . to cut down trees.

Kintaro and his . . . . . lived in a very lonely part of . . . . . forest. There was no village near, and . . . . . only people they ever saw were the . . . . . . Kintaro, however, was not lonely. Because he . . . . . no other children to play with, he . . . . . friends with the animals. He often played . . . . . them, and soon he learned how to . . . . . to them. The animals loved and respected . . . . . because he was stronger and cleverer than . . . . . of them. His best friends were the . . . . ., the deer, the monkey and the hare. . . . . . had great fun playing together.

. . . .
. . . .
. . . .
. . . .
. . . .
. . . .
. . . .
. . . .
. . . .
. . . .
. . . .
. . . .
. . . .
. . . .
. . . .
. . . .
. . . .
. . . .
. . . .
. . . .
. . . .
. . . .
. . . .
. . . .

Princess Moonlight p1, Takashi Shimaoka
(Macmillan 'Rangers' Range 5)

4 The students should try to work out what the missing words are and write them in the margin, trying to complete every blank and putting only one word in each blank. Don't time the test but give each student a chance to try every word. The principle underlying cloze procedure is that the number of correctly guessed words indicates how well the student can reconstruct the author's message by using knowledge of structure, by predicting from the context and by choosing words which 'fit' best with the author's own choice of vocabulary and language patterns.

5 Mark the passages by giving one mark for each correct answer or for an answer which is synonymous or closely fits the structure and style of the text.

6 Turn the marks into percentages and compare the percentages for students.

7 The percentages can be interpreted roughly as in Figure 6.

Figure 6 Interpretation of cloze scores

%	Level	Significance for the student	Advice about the book
60% and over	independent level	should be able to work successfully on his own	this book is the right level for unsupported extensive reading
40-60%	instructional level	he will need teacher support	best to find an easier book
below 40%	frustrational level	a good deal of teacher support would be needed and difficulty would be experienced even then	very unwise to use this book

This guide should be used in conjunction with the teacher's judgement, experience and growing knowledge of the students. Check the test scores with a general assessment of the students' other work. Better students should have higher scores and scores should be similar among students who do equally well in classwork.

For a teacher who wants to set up a class library with a new class for whom no reading records are available, cloze tests can be used to get an idea of the range of levels appropriate to the class.

1 Make a rough assessment of a general level for the class from a scheme of graded Readers.
2 Put together a collection of Readers around that level, including some from above and below the level.
3 Prepare cloze tests on a cross-section of texts in the way described above and administer them to the class.

This will give a rough estimation of where each student can usefully begin reading and where he will begin to experience difficulty.

Cloze procedure is a useful device for helping a teacher to choose appropriate books, as long as it is applied to well-written books with motivating subject matter and as long as it is used in conjunction with the students' known reading interests.

3.4 Technical presentation

The process of reading can be considerably assisted by the technical presentation of a book. So a final set of factors for any teacher to consider when selecting graded Readers are things not specifically to do with the text itself, such as front covers, size and variety of print, the use of headings and subheadings and the relationship between artwork and text.

3.4.1 *Front covers*

The importance of front covers is not to be underestimated, especially with younger learners. The appearance of the front cover often seems to be the main reason why a child picks up a book. This is why, if a class library can be put together, it is so important to display books. Many graded Readers now look like 'real' books on the outside, and on turning the pages, colourful illustrative material makes them appealing and varied. The Longman 'Movieworld' and 'Galaxies' series provide good examples of this.

3.4.2 *Illustrations*

As well as being a factor in motivation, illustrations are an aid to comprehension, so the teacher should always check their clarity. In some books at the elementary level, for example *The Sky's the Limit* ('Heinemann Guided Readers' Beginner) illustrations actually take over the telling of the story and allow expression of more complex ideas. Pictures have the capacity to convey much of the emotion, characterisation, background etc that is implicit in the text but which cannot be expressed openly in the controlled language. In more advanced Readers, for example *Animals Dangerous to Man* ('Longman Structural Readers' Stage 5) a combination of line drawings, maps, diagrams and some very good close-up photographs helps students to follow the information in the text.

3.4.3 *Page by page presentation*

There are now many graded Readers, both fiction and non-fiction, which have a rather more varied format than continuous prose text.

They present different types of text and other graphic or non-verbal ways of presenting information. This kind of book can be usefully included in a class library or chosen as a class Reader where other reading sources in English are meagre. They introduce students to different kinds of writing and give them opportunities to interpret such devices as graphs, charts and diagrams. For example, *Johnny Ring* (Macmillan 'Rangers' Range 4) is a good adventure story which also contains songs, maps, historical notes, biographical details, period photographs and clear illustrations to accompany the text which give a 'feel' of the time in which the story is set. Similar 'fact panels' are included in other 'Rangers' such as *Bluestones, Appleby Fair, The Minoan Cup* and *Police Patrol.* The 'Longman Structural Readers' Analysis series of non-fiction Readers, such as *Fair Play, Your Choice* and *A Woman's Place?* also provides excellent examples of this type of book.

3.4.4 *Graphics*

A teacher needs to look for books which give readers lots of help in following information. Reading can be described as the reconstruction of the writer's message in the mind of the reader and it follows that a method of presentation which helps the reader to make an effective reconstruction is a great advantage. It is useful to check graded Readers to see how they organise material to make it more accessible to the reader. This may be done in various ways.

(a) Clear, attractive typeface is important but the size of print must be appropriate to the reader, not too large and not too small.

(b) Variations in type assist comprehension. For example, in *It Never Snows in England* ('Longman Structural Readers' Stage 1) the thoughts of the main character are italicised. In *Modern British Painting* (Hart-Davis Educational) the names of the artists are picked out in bolder type.

(c) Subheadings focus the attention of the reader on content in advance and help to guide him through the organisation of material. Edward Arnold's 'Leaders Series' is particularly good at doing this in books like *Dangermen* and *Hollywood Monsters*. And a book like *Your Choice?* ('Longman Structural Readers' Grade 5) shows how subheadings can help a reader to predict content. Chapter 2 guides the reader through the organisation of the subject matter by the use of the following headings:

> **Background to advertising**
> Something old, something new . . .
> What do advertisements do?
> From the usual . . .
> . . . to the unusual
> The special case of television and radio advertising
> Who organises advertising?
> What do advertising agencies do?
> Agencies and their target groups.

All of the above factors — covers, lay-out, illustrations and graphics — need to be looked at and assessed by any teacher making a selection of Readers, not just from the point of view of motivation but also because the task of reading itself can be made easier by these factors.

3.5 A personal questionnaire

To summarise the various issues raised in the preceding pages, Figure 7 is a questionnaire for the individual teacher. The idea is that any teacher who has a degree of freedom in selecting Readers, whether as a class set or for a class library, should consider the following questions.

Figure 7 A questionnaire for the teacher

1 What are the characteristics of my class as a group?
   — How big is the group?
   — What is the age range?
   — What is the mixture of sexes?

2 What do I know about my students as individuals?
   — What kind of cultural background do they come from?
   — What experience of reading in English do they already have?
   — What are their personal preferences in reading?

3 What do I know about the reading abilities of my students?
   — Have my students completed any tests I might have access to?
   — Can another teacher give me useful information?
   — Are there any reading records I might refer to?

4 What do I know about the language level of the books?
   — Is there a scheme which sets out the number of headwords?
   — How frequently are new words introduced?
   — Does the publisher explain how the level matches
     (a) student competence or
     (b) main course material?
   — Can I make a quick appraisal of a book using a rough method?
   — Can I use a simple 'readability' test with my class?

5 How appropriate are the books for my students?
   — Do I know the age range the book is intended for?
   — Has another teacher used this book and was it popular
     with the students?
   — Does the content interest and motivate me?
   — What is the cultural setting of the book and how easily
     will my students be able to appreciate it?
   — Does the book contain a glossary?

6 Is the book well-presented?
   — Are the illustrations (including the cover) attractive
     and appropriate?
   — Is the size of print and format of the pages
     appropriate?
   — Does the general layout of the book offer help in
     understanding?

4 Introducing graded Readers

4.1 When to introduce graded Readers

In the very early stages of language learning, any reading activities should be closely integrated with the development of other skills such as listening. This is because students need to become familiar with the correspondence between the sounds they hear and the symbols on the printed page and with how those symbols are ordered into words and sentences. The major implication is that students should only read what they have already heard and the material of the main course book is probably sufficient for this purpose of familiarisation.

The length of this stage will depend on the intensity of the course but, as soon as the students have mastered a few hundred words of English and a range of simple structures, graded Readers can be used to support learning and encourage good reading habits. Because the structures and most of the lexical items are familiar, students can engage in fluent reading and build up confidence.

The point was made in Chapter 3 that teachers can select judiciously among books available at the lowest level in series of graded Readers to find simple, motivating 'conversational' material in the form of cartoon dialogue or dramatic script, often very well illustrated. Both the illustration and the immediacy of the dialogue form encourage direct reading rather than word by word translation.

At the other end of the scale, with advanced learners, teachers need to decide at what level to introduce authentic reading matter, unedited novels, short stories and non-fiction books. These can be introduced gradually into intensive reading lessons in extract form, selected according to appropriacy of level. Unedited books can be introduced into a class library and some students encouraged to try them. The important thing is to remember that the ultimate goal of a reading programme is to encourage independence in reading, and teachers should be on the lookout for books which would be accessible to students in unedited form. A team of teachers working together can build up a useful reference list of these.

4.2 Preparing learners for extensive reading

There are two important ways in which students need preparation for extensive reading. Firstly, they can be prepared psychologically. This means, for example, encouraging them to think about their own approaches to reading. Secondly, they can be trained methodologically in some of the strategies needed for effective reading.

4.2.1 Psychological preparation

Talking to students about their reading is one way of preparing students 'psychologically' for reading extensively in a foreign language. The teacher can ask students what they read in their first language, how often they read, what sorts of books they enjoy most. And questions can be asked about their attempts to read in English too. In small classes these questions can form the basis of informal discussion, either in the first language or English, whichever is most appropriate to the group, the teacher and the level of competence in English.

Alternatively the teacher can make a questionnaire. This could be used for an individual reading and writing task or it could be used for speaking practice with students interviewing one another in pairs. Information gained from any of these activities can be used in different ways: to guide the selection of Readers for a class library;

to exploit a common group interest in choosing a set of class Readers or to help students choose books for their private reading. It is worth bearing in mind that the answers to the questionnaire may not be fully reliable because students often say things to impress, or give answers they feel will be acceptable to the teacher. However, finding out about reading interests generally has positive results and gives the teacher useful insights.

Figure 8 is an example of a reading interest questionnaire. It has been used very successfully with groups of adult intermediate students. One way of using the questionnaire is to follow these steps.

1 The teacher introduces the activity by asking the class the questions in section B and eliciting answers from individual students, building up types of reading material and types of books on the blackboard and checking that students understand them. Like this:

Reading material	Types of books	
newspapers	sport	crime
magazines	love stories	adventure
comics	history	mysteries
novels	biographies	spy thrillers
non fiction	science fiction	. . . .
. . . .	. . . .	. . . .

2 The teacher gives out the questionnaire and asks students to read quietly through the questions and write down their answers.
3 The teacher asks students to work in pairs and interview each other, asking and answering the questions in sections A to D.
4 The teacher collects in the questionnaires and collates the information.

In step 3 the students can be encouraged to say as much as possible, using their written answers as prompts. The teacher can monitor the pair work, listening to different pairs and picking up as much useful information as possible.

The questionnaire can be adapted and made simpler for lower level classes. For example, the questions in section B could be set out as follows.

What do you like to read about? Tick (✓)

☐	history	☐	animals
☐	science fiction	☐	sport
☐	adventure	☐	crime
☐	love	☐	travel
☐	family life	☐	politics

Figure 8 A Reading Questionnaire

Ask your friend about his/her reading:
(Read all of the questionnaire *before* you start to ask and answer the questions)

SECTION A: Personal details

1 What's your name? ....
2 Where are you from? ....
3 What's your first language? ....
4 Do you speak any other language? ....

SECTION B: Reading in your FIRST language

1 What sort of things do you read in .... (first language)?
   ....
   (eg newspapers, magazines, novels, comics, non-fiction)

2   What do you like to read about in . . . . (first language)?
. . . . (eg sport, politics, science, love, animals)

SECTION C: Reading in ENGLISH

1   What *sort* of things do you read/would you like to read in
    English? . . . . (eg stories, comics, newspapers,
    women's magazines, technical materials, business reports)

2   What do you/would you like to read *about* in English? . . . .
    . . . . (eg travel, food, literature, the Queen, football,
    engineering)

SECTION D: Special problems

When you're reading English, are any of these a problem for you?

	Yes, it's a big problem	Sometimes yes Sometimes no	No, it isn't a problem	I don't know
1 reading too slowly				
2 understanding new words				
3 making lists of new words				
4 remembering new words				
5 understanding sentences				
6 grammar				
7 pronunciation				
8 translating into your language				
9 using a bilingual dictionary				
10 using an English dictionary				

SECTION E: Self-Assessment: What do you think about your reading in English?

Finally, do you think you are (tick the right box):

> ★ a good reader ☐ or a bad reader? ☐
> ★ a quick reader ☐ or a slow reader? ☐
> ★ a careful reader ☐ or a careless reader? ☐

SECTION F

FINALLY . . .
is there anything else you would like me to know about your interests and abilities in English, or in reading:

eg — would you like me to try to find some newspapers, magazines or books on special topics?

— would you like me to work out some vocabulary, grammar or pronunciation exercises on reading?

— would you like me to find some books by famous authors in English literature?

Norman Whitney
Ealing College of Higher Education   Thank you!

Preparing learners 'psychologically' for extensive reading can also involve developing awareness of their own learning problems. This is included in section D in the questionnaire and talking about all of these points whenever possible can help students to understand their own role in reading, what successful reading involves and what strategies they can actively train themselves to adopt.

4.2.2 *Methodological preparation*

The 'strategies' just mentioned would ideally be taught and trained in the intensive part of a reading programme. This is where the point made in the Introduction to this book is so important — that in the development of fluent reading in a foreign language, intensive and extensive reading practice are mutually dependent. Intensive reading lessons provide students with training in the strategies and skills they need to become successful readers. Extensive reading provides opportunities for putting that training into practice independently, at an unsupported level of learning. It is vital, if extensive reading is to be a valuable, confidence-building activity, one which develops good reading habits, that students are well-prepared before they begin.

Figure 9 shows the components of an ideal intensive reading plan and the way these feed the extensive reading programme. Information on all of these components can be found in another book in this series (Williams 1984). It is worth taking up three of the strategies here and showing how the teacher can encourage students in very concrete ways, to employ them in extensive reading.

(a) Using dictionaries

Ideally a learner will be encouraged to use a dictionary as a final strategy in working out meaning. In order to develop fluent direct reading rather than constant translation, students can be trained to exploit the normal strategies they would use in working out the meaning of an unfamiliar word in their mother tongue. In other words, they would look at the general context, make an intelligent guess from the structure and content of the sentence, study the structure of the word to see if suffixes or prefixes give clues to meaning, or try to relate it to similar words.

Once students have tried these strategies, the dictionary can be a check on a meaning arrived at tentatively. In many instances, however, it will be the only efficient method of finding out the meaning of a new word. But reference to a dictionary will only be helpful if the learners have experience of using it and training in the necessary skills. Children certainly need training and a surprising number of adult students need help too, especially when dealing with English-English, ie monolingual dictionaries. It sometimes proves difficult to wean learners away from bilingual dictionaries but these can create problems. Firstly, they have to be very detailed to do the job properly. Secondly, constant use of a bilingual dictionary encourages word-for-word translation during reading and hinders the development of fluent reading. It is helpful to encourage students to get into the habit of using a bilingual dictionary only after trying a monolingual dictionary. The latter, if specially written for foreign students and at an appropriate level, is the best kind for students to use as an aid to extensive reading.

There are at least three skills needed to use a dictionary efficiently, depending on the amount and kind of information it gives, and all three can be trained through various types of exercises:

- Exercises in learning the sequence of the alphabet, arranging words by sequence of second, third and fourth letters and so on, using guide words at the top of the page will practise location skills.
- Exercises in using the pronunciation key of a particular dictionary will ensure that students can exploit information on how to pronounce new words.
- Exercises in selecting from several meanings the one which fits the particular context will ensure that students can distinguish among multiple meanings given in the dictionary.

All of these exercise types can be found in a number of books produced to accompany dictionaries. For example, *Use Your Dictionary* is a practice book for users of the *Oxford Advanced Learners' Dictionary of Current English*. Other useful practice books are Macmillan's *Working with Words from A Learner's First Dictionary* and *Working with Words from the New Basic Dictionary* and *Learning with Longman's Dictionary of Contemporary English*. The Teachers' Guide to the

Figure 9 The relationship between intensive and extensive reading

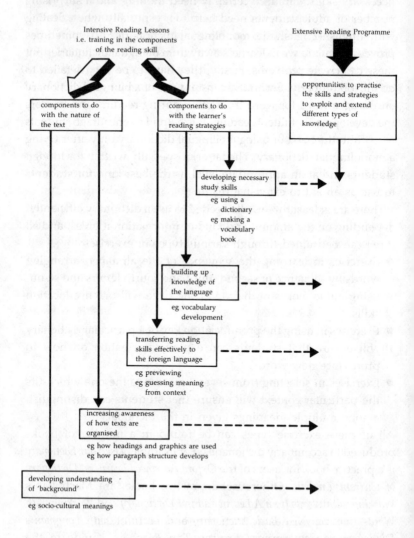

Intensive Reading Lessons
i.e. training in the components
of the reading skill

Extensive Reading Programme

opportunities to practise
the skills and strategies
to exploit and extend
different types of
knowledge

components to do
with the nature of
the text

components to do
with the learner's
reading strategies

developing necessary
study skills

eg using a
dictionary
eg making a
vocabulary
book

building up
knowledge of
the language

eg vocabulary
development

transferring reading
skills effectively to
the foreign language

eg previewing
eg guessing meaning
from context

increasing awareness
of how texts are
organised

eg how headings and graphics are used
eg how paragraph structure develops

developing understanding
of 'background'

eg socio-cultural meanings

Longman dictionary also has good exercises on alphabetical order, understanding the definitions and using the grammatical codes.

As well as initial training, students need as much dictionary practice as possible in the classroom. There are strong arguments for schools and institutions to provide sets of dictionaries for classroom reference. However, even when the only dictionary in the classroom is the teacher's own, it is best used by students to check meanings for themselves rather than as a source for a quick teacher explanation.

(b) Making vocabulary books

Keeping a personal vocabulary book, building up its content with words learned during reading and using it for reference during writing tasks can be a valuable learning strategy. Students can be encouraged to keep individual notebooks into which they copy new words they find useful and want to remember. This is best done after a period of reading so that it does not intrude on the reading itself.

One way of encouraging the idea of keeping such books is to talk informally with the class. Figure 10 is part of a questionnaire that the author used with her class of Cambridge First Certificate students. It led to a useful exchange of learning strategies among the students and some were encouraged by others to try new ways of doing things.

Figure 10 Part of a questionnaire on vocabulary books

1 Do you have a vocabulary book?

2 Which words do you put in it?
   — words you read out of class?
   — words you learn from the teacher in class?
   — words you learn from texts in class?

3 How do you arrange the words?
  — as you learn them or read them?
  — day by day or lesson by lesson?
  — under topics?
  — alphabetically?

4 What do you actually write in your vocabulary book?
  — just the word?
  — its translation into your first language?
  — a synonym in English?
  — other parts of speech?
  — sentences which show how the word is used?
  — its pronunciation? How?

Certainly, in encouraging students to make personal vocabulary books, it would be wise to show them ways of including the last three items in question 4. If students are not able to use phonetic transcription, at least an indication of word stress is useful so they can be taught ways of marking this (Figure 11).

Figure 11 Ways of marking word stress

Method 1	**Method 2**	**Method 3**
import	impórt	import
imagination	imaginátion	imagination
cigarette	cigarétte	cigarette
depart	depárt	depart

Writing out a whole sentence from the text to remember how a word is used is also important to avoid the danger of misremembered meanings.

(c) Previewing a book
One of the strategies employed by a reader in his first language, when choosing a book to read, is to preview it, in other words to look at

the title, look at the cover, read any 'blurb' on the back cover about the story or the writer, look at the list of contents or chapter headings and glance through the book to get an impression of the lay-out, the size of print, the illustrations and so on. A preview can 'whet the appetite', increase interest and strengthen the motivation to read. We often preview books quite unconsciously when we read books in our first language.

The teacher can exploit this natural tendency to preview by encouraging students to think for a while before reading. Specific ways of doing this with the whole class before setting out on a class Reader are discussed in Chapter 7. When individuals choose from a class library, the teacher can adopt the same approach by setting up pair work interviews about 'first impressions'. Figure 12 shows an activity for pair work with a group of adult intermediate students. The interview recorded here is between two Italians, Sylvia and Nadia.

Figure 12 FIRST IMPRESSIONS   (Previewing)

Ask your friend about his/her "first impressions" of the book he/she has chosen.

A Facts about the book
QUESTIONS   **TO HELP YOU**

1 What's the title of your book?   look at the front cover

   [The title is 'Silas Marner']

2 Who's the author?   look at the front cover

   [The author is George Eliot]

3 Who's the publisher?   look at the front or
                                           back cover
   [It's Alpha Classics. The pub-
   lisher is Oxford University Press]

4 When was it published?

[It was published in 1979]

look inside the front cover — give the first or most recent date

5 Do you know the ISBN number?

[YES, the number is 0194241831]

look inside — or on the back cover!

B First thoughts and reactions
QUESTIONS

TO HELP YOU

1 What does the title suggest to you?

[I think it's a name-a man's name]

eg type of story (drama, love, history)

2 Does the author's name mean anything to you?

[Yes, I know... I think he's an important English writer]

eg famous, alive/dead, British/American

3 What do you think it will be about?

[I think it will be- it's a story about old times.]

eg sport, geography, entertainment, literature

4 Do you think you'll find it interesting or boring?

[I think I'll find it interesting]

eg yes/quite/very

5 Do you think you'll find it easy? or difficult?

[Quite easy]

eg very/OK/too

C Ideas about Reading
QUESTIONS

TO HELP YOU

1 When will you be able to read
  your book?

  [*In the evenings*]

eg each day/on
Sunday

2 How long do you think it will
  take you to read it?

  [*I think about 2 or 3 days*]

eg X hrs, X days

3 Will you try to read it quickly
  or slowly?

  [*I'll try to read it quickly*]

eg quickly/slowly/
don't know

4 Do you think you will like or
  dislike the book?

  [*I think I will like it*]

eg yes/no/don't
know/hope so

Thanks!
Enjoy your reading!

Norman Whitney

4.3 Integrating Readers and reading activities

Many teachers have now integrated extensive reading successfully
into their teaching programmes. The sorts of decisions they have had
to take are these.

How to organise the use of graded Readers.

How much time to spend on extensive reading.

How to link extensive reading to the main course.

4.3.1 *How to organise the use of graded Readers*

To begin with the first point above, there are perhaps two alternative
methods for organising extensive reading.

(a) Individual reading from a class library

Many teachers now feel that the most effective way of using graded Readers is through individualised silent reading. Ideally this will be with a small class library. With the advice of a teacher if necessary, students can select books, according to their own reading interests and abilities, to take away and read at their own pace at home or in reading periods.

This situation is obviously 'ideal' in the sense that in reality teachers are constrained by availability of space, time, equipment and finance. The lack of these resources may present problems in organising a class library but the undoubted success that many teachers achieve with class libraries is an incentive to do whatever is possible to promote individualised private reading (see Appendix III on Library Boxes in the Malaysian reading scheme). Even more difficult is the problem that private reading time in class, accompanied by individual tutorial sessions to advise and assist students, may be radically different from teaching approaches which traditionally occur in a particular situation. Extensive reading may not be encouraged as an 'in-school' activity in some educational systems. For example, research in Britain (Lunzer and Gardner 1977) showed that secondary school students in general have little opportunity to read and many teachers are reluctant to spend time on reading because they are afraid it will be misused. In such situations the English teacher's initial task will be to persuade colleagues and authorities to regard extensive reading as a useful language activity to be encouraged in the classroom, especially where students are not likely to have resources for reading at home. Students will also need careful persuasion and preparation in new, more independent ways of learning. Primarily they will need to be convinced of the advantages to themselves of private reading in a foreign language.

What are these advantages?
- Firstly, if private reading is contrasted with the traditional methods of reading aloud by the teacher or by good students, or even

'reading round the class', it has the considerable advantage of letting students read at their own pace. Individual reading enables them to apply to English the skills and strategies they employ in reading their own language. No two people learn a language at the same rate or in exactly the same way, and the same is true of reading. Extensive silent reading gives students the chance to vary their pace and their approach according to the way they interact with particular parts of a text. For example, a student may choose to skim through several pages to get a preview of what comes next, or check back with something he has read earlier to ensure that he has understood. He may stop for a while and think about something or he may read the same paragraph several times to make sure he grasps the meaning accurately. If students are prepared for reading in the ways suggested earlier and are given the opportunity to employ these strategies, they learn to read for general meaning without frequent stops to look words up in the dictionary. Also, by reading silently at their own pace, they can develop the ability to deduce the meanings of words and phrases from clues in the context.

- This kind of individual and self-directed process makes students independent in learning, which is an important factor in success. Traditional classrooms, with the teacher firmly in control of all activity and with the teacher's voice as the focus of attention, tend to remove responsibility from students for their own progress. This is the point made by two writers on autonomous learning (Henner-Stanchina and Riley 1978: 78) when they say:

> Many adults are convinced that all they have to do to learn a language is to attend a course. Simple bodily presence is all that is required of them: they will sit in the classroom, the teacher will do his job, and somehow, learning will take place.

But, of course, students can only learn by being actively involved in learning.

- Individual silent reading has the further advantage of allowing students to choose books according to their own interests and experience. Students may have very different reasons for reading in a foreign language. In an intermediate class of girls, for example, one student may want to see if she can enjoy a thriller in English and pick up *Death at the Wedding* (Nelson 'Streamline Readers'). Another may be curious about a foreign culture or a country she would like to visit and select *Visiting the USA* (Macmillan 'Rangers'). Yet another may be interested in comparing social issues in Britain and her own country, such as the role of women, and pick up *Women in Britain* ('Evans Graded Reading').

A class library then, gives students the opportunity to read books of their own choice. Individual private reading is a way of organising language learning which recognises that students have different experiences, interests, motivation, intellectual capacities, tastes and levels of maturity. Success in developing reading skills depends on respecting and allowing for these differences.

(b) Using a class Reader

This is the traditional and still popular method, using multiple copies of the same Reader as a class set. It has several advantages, which will be discussed more fully in Chapter 7.

- The teacher can prepare the class thoroughly for reading, 'warming up' to the story, providing background information and key language and thereby developing motivation.

- It is much easier to give support during reading, to take key passages for more intensive study and to check how well students understand the story.

- Weaker students receive maximum help, for example by listening to the teacher reading parts of the story out loud, or to a cassette, or by working in a small remedial group with the teacher.

- The teacher, through questioning or discussion, can encourage creative thinking and critical evaluation. When students are children, this is an important element in their general education, and the English lesson can make a valuable contribution by helping them to analyse their reading experience and to respect imagination and intellect.

● Graded Readers can also be exploited for more intensive classwork. They are an extra resource for the teacher to draw on. This point is taken up in Chapter 8.

4.3.2 *How much time to spend on extensive reading*

It is often possible, with a class Reader, for students to take the book home and do reading homework and, when the class library method is used, students should be able to take books home and read as much as they wish. However, it is not always possible for books to be taken from the school premises and, in this case, time for reading in class is vital. It is also desirable, from the point of view of setting good reading habits, to spend class time on extensive reading.

The appropriate amount of time to spend on reading will clearly depend on the overall amount of time in an English course and the intensity of a course. For example, in a general school curriculum where students have five hours of English every week, one hour a fortnight for a class Reader or for individual private reading and related activities would be useful. With part-time adult students taking eight hours a week, one hour every week might prove successful.

4.3.3 *How to link extensive reading to the main course*

Links can be built with the general English programme in a number of ways, for example, introducing Readers related to topics in the course book or using the beginning of a new class Reader for listening work or intensive reading. These possibilities will be discussed in detail in Chapter 5. Where a class library is used, the teacher can refer to particular books at various points in the main programme, picking out links with the course book through character types, settings, situations and topics and recommending the books to students who might be interested. If a course book is in general use in a school or institution, teachers can co-operate to produce the kind of list of which part is shown in Figure 13. This was put together over a year by a group of teachers using O'Neill's *Kernel Lessons Intermediate* (Longman) and served as a reference guide, with updatings and additions for a couple of years.

Figure 13 Integrating Readers into the Scheme of Work

Topic	Readers	Series	Publisher's level	Headword level
Unit 1 Ordinary People Texts 1-6 on presentation pages	The African Child	'Collins Graded Readers'	Level 4	1500
	A Town Like Alice	'Heinemann Guided Readers'	Intermediate	1600
	Women in Britain	'Evans Graded Readers'	Grade 4	1000
	Tom Sawyer	Nelson 'Streamline'		2000
	Old Mali and the Boy	'Heinemann Guided Readers'	Intermediate	1600
	The Snow Goose	'Heinemann Guided Readers'	Intermediate	1600
Unit 2 Escape Episode of The Man Who Escaped	The Runaways	'Heinemann Guided Readers'	Elementary	1100
	The Wooden Horse	'Longman Simplified English Series'		2000
	The Space Invaders	'Heinemann Guided Readers'	Intermediate	1600
	Alive	OUP 'Alpha'		1500
	The Thirty Nine Steps	'Longmann Structural Readers'	Stage 4	1100
	Walkabout	'Heinemann Guided Readers'	Intermediate	1600
	Means of Escape	Nelson 'Getaway'	Intermediate	
Unit 3 Marriage Texts 5 and 6 on presentation pages	Elephant Walk	'Heinemann Guided Readers'	Intermediate	1600
	My Cousin Rachel	'Heinemann Guided Readers'	Intermediate	1600
	Rebecca	'Heinemann Guided Readers'	Upper	2200
	Desirée, wife of Marshall Bernadotte	'Longman Structural Readers'	Stage 4	1100
Unit 4 Biography Text presentation pages	Great People of our Time	Macmillan 'Rangers'	Range 6	2200
	More People of our Time	Macmillan 'Rangers'	Range 6	2200
	Some Unusual People	'Longman Structural Readers'	Stage 2	500
	Six Great Scientists	Macmillan 'Rangers'	Range 6	2200
	Famous Women of the Twentieth Century	Macmillan 'Rangers'	Range 7	2700

Unit 5 Baking and Cooking Text 2 on presentation pages	A Taste of Britain What's Cooking?	'Longman Structural Readers' 'Evans Graded Readers'	Stage 4 Grade 5	1100 2300

Unit 6
Detection
Episode of
The Man
Who
Escaped
	Trent's Last Case
	The Woman Who
	  Disappeared
	Inspector Ghote Breaks
	  an Egg
	The Queen of Death
	Seven Detective Stories
	
	Kojak: The Trade Off
		Nelson 'Streamline'
		'Heinemann Guided Readers'
		
		'Collins Graded Readers'
		
		'Heinemann Guided Readers'
		Longman 'New Method
		  Supplementary Readers'
		'Longman Simplified English
		  Series'
			Intermediate
			Intermediate
			
			Level 6
			
			Intermediate
			Stage 5
				2000
				1600
				
				2500
				
				1600
				1800
				
				2000

Unit 7 Interests and Hobbies Texts 1, 2, 3 on presentation pages	Modern British Painting Clothes and Fashion Theatre in Britain The Story of Pop	Hart Davis Educational 'Evans Graded Readers' 'Evans Graded Readers' 'Heinemann Guided Readers'	low intermediate Grade 4 Grade 3 Upper Level	 1100 800 2200

Unit 8
Sports
Texts 2 and 4
on
presentation
pages
	Fair Play
	
	Motor Racing
	The Olympics
	How Sport and Games
	  Began
	The Olympic Games
		'Longman Supplementary
		  Readers'
		'Cassell Spotlight Readers'
		'Cassell Spotlight Readers'
		'Evans Graded Readers'
		
		'Heinemann Guided Readers'
			Stage 4
			
			Level 3
			Level 4
			Grade 2
			
			Upper
				1100
				
				1050
				1400
				700
				
				2200

Unit 9 The Space Age and Science Fiction Text 1 on presentation pages	Exploring Space Me, Myself and I A Fall of Moondust Rendezvous with Rama I, Robot	Macmillan 'Rangers' 'Longman Structural Readers' Nelson 'Streamline' OUP 'Alpha' OUP 'Alpha'	Range 5 Stage 4 Intermediate	1850 + 1100 2000 1000 1000
Unit 10 Romance Text 5 on presentation pages	The Valentine Generation Love Story Jane Eyre Ulster Story David and Marianne	'Longman Structural Readers' OUP 'Alpha' 'Collins Graded Readers' 'Longman Structural Readers' 'Longman Structural Readers'	Stage 5 Level 4 Stage 3 Stage 3	1500 1500 1500 750 750

Unit 11
Football
Text 5 on
presentation
pages
	Football
	Football
	The Goalkeeper's
	  Revenge
	My Life and the
	  Beautiful Game
		'Evans Graded Readers'
		'Heinemann Guided Readers'
		'Heinemann Guided Readers'
		
		OUP 'Alpha'
			Grade 5
			Intermediate
			Elementary
				2300
				1600
				1100
				
				1000

Unit 12 Murder Episode of The Man who Escaped	Death at the Wedding Nothing is the Number When You Die Bonecrack Bristol Murder	Nelson 'Streamline' 'Collins Graded Readers' Nelson 'Getaway' 'Heinemann Guided Readers'	Intermediate Level 4 Intermediate	2000 1500 1600

Unit 13 Horror	The Story of Frankenstein	Macmillan 'Rangers'	Range 4	1500
Texts 1 and 2 on presentation pages	The Birds and Other Stories	'Longman Structural Readers'	Stage 4	1100
	Jaws	Longman 'Movieworld'		
	Dracula	'Heinemann Guided Readers'	Intermediate	1600
	Hollywood Monsters	Edward Arnold 'Leaders'	Intermediate	
Unit 14 Cinema	Star Wars	Longman 'Movieworld'		500
Episode of The Man who Escaped	Cinema Stunts	'Collins Graded Readers'	Level 3	1000
	The Cinema	'Heinemann Guided Readers'	Upper	2200
	Cinema	'Cassell Spotlight Readers'	Level 5	1750
Unit 15 Transport	Modern Methods of Transport	'Cassell Scientific Readers'	Level 3/4	1400
Text 1 of presentation pages and conversation	Airports	'Cassell Spotlight Readers'	Level 3	1050
	The Story of Trains	'Oxford Graded Readers'	Pre-intermediate	1000
	Airport International	'Collins Graded Readers'	Level 4	1500
Unit 16 Travelling	Visiting the USA	Macmillan 'Rangers'	Range 5	1850 +
Text 5 on presentation pages	A Journey through Japan	Macmillan 'Rangers'	Range 5	1850 +
Unit 17 Britain	Family Life	'Evans Graded Readers'	Grade 4	1100
Conversation	Town or Country	Hart-Davis 'Insights'	Intermediate	
	Oxford and Cambridge	'Heinemann Guided Readers'	Elementary	1100
	Great British Ghosts	'Longman Structural Readers'	Stage 3	750
	The Book of British Humour	'Longman Structural Readers'	Stage 4	1100
	Fleet Street	'Cassell Spotlight Readers'	Level 4	1400
Unit 18 The Army and War	Johnny Ring	Macmillan 'Rangers'	Range 4	1500
	The Moon is Down	'Heinemann Guided Readers'	Intermediate	1600
Text 1 on presentation pages	Company K	Nelson 'Getaway'	Intermediate	
	The Guns of Navarone	'Collins Graded Readers'	Level 5	2000
	The Eagle has Landed	'Collins Graded Readers'	Level 5	2000
Unit 19 Inventions	Electricity	Macmillan 'Base Books'	Intermediate	
Conversation	Five Great Inventors	Macmillan 'Rangers'	Range 6	2200
	Six Great Scientists	Macmillan 'Rangers'	Range 6	2200
	Your car and how it works	'Longman Structural Readers'	Stage 4	1100
	Inventions	'Cassell Spotlight Readers'	Level 2	700
	Computers	'Longman Structural Readers'	Stage 4	1100
Unit 20 The Wild West	The Wild West	'Evans Graded Readers'	Grade 4	1100
Text 2 on presentation pages	True Grit	OUP 'Alpha'		1000
	Comanche	OUP 'Alpha'		1000
	Shane	'Heinemann Guided Readers'	Intermediate	1600
	Clint Magee	'Longman Structural Readers'	Stage 3	750

5 The Class library

Teachers who choose to set up a class library to encourage extensive reading need to consider a number of practical issues: how to organise the library; how to keep useful records of reading; and finally, how to direct and encourage students' choice of books.

5.1 Organising the library

Organising a class library takes time, enthusiasm and commitment from the teacher. On the other hand, if students take part in the organisation, it can be a very productive activity. There are a number of steps involved in establishing a class library: choosing books, displaying them, classifying them for students and working out a borrowing system.

5.1.1 Choosing books

The first task is to assemble as many books as possible, using the various criteria listed in Chapter 3. It is sometimes the case that students themselves, particularly adult students, can be involved in choosing books for a library. In situations where students are expected to buy their own course books, in private language schools for example, and where they have access to bookshops selling graded Readers, students can be asked to contribute a couple of Readers each, ones which appeal to them personally and which they think their classmates may be interested in as well. These books can form the core of a library. This is a method which has proved popular and effective in language schools in Britain.

If the teachers themselves are selecting books from a bookshop or a publisher's catalogue, they can use students' reading interest questionnaires for guidance, as discussed in the previous chapter. They can also use their knowledge of previously popular books and their sensitivity to the needs and interests of their students.

If the English staff of an institution can work together on the setting up of class libraries, this is the arrangement with by far the greatest potential for success. The task of selecting, ordering and 'vetting' books can be shared. For example, different teachers can each take new books to read and prepare self-access materials for them, in the way described later in Chapter 6.

5.1.2 Displaying books

The best way a teacher can create interest in the library and a good atmosphere for reading is to make a conscious effort to promote books. In a situation where teachers or the students have their own classrooms, the library can be a permanent feature, set up in a colourful 'book corner', on an open bookcase, with an attractive display of books and a wall display of relevant and interesting material. Publishers sometimes provide information about Readers in the form of wallcharts, and brochures can be pinned on the wall, too. But, more effectively, students' work related to their reading can be displayed. Students of all ages seem to enjoy looking at each other's work. Book reviews, letters to the author, book cover designs, when mounted on coloured paper, make attractive and interesting display materials. For teachers who are not fortunate enough to have this kind of facility, a large cardboard box, easy to move and store, is probably the best way of housing the book collection. Books can then be displayed quickly on a desk for access.

5.1.3 *Classifying books*

Deciding whether to classify books and exactly what kind of classification to use needs careful thought. Some teachers may feel that students are well able to choose Readers of an appropriate level for themselves, and that if students tend to choose books which are too easy for them, then nothing is lost, because they are still reading extensively and improving their fluency. Other teachers may want to indicate the level of books in some way to help students who aim too high. In such a case a student may pick up a book that looks interesting but the teacher may feel that, despite high motivation, the student will have to decipher the text laboriously rather than read it and will consequently be frustrated by the level of difficulty and perhaps lose confidence.

Level can be indicated for the students by marking the books with a circle of coloured gummed paper in a corner of the cover or a coloured strip across the spine. If books are carefully marked in this way, they can still be displayed according to type: thrillers, technical books, biographies etc, so that 'content' rather than 'level' is presented to students. But the system of colour coding for level also ensures that students always know what they can read with a fair expectation of success. This is particularly important with students whose confidence is slow to develop. Using a coding system to help students choose books is potentially far more successful than if the teacher chooses books for individuals, a process which can dampen enthusiasm and deprive students of the pleasurable activity of browsing.

5.1.4 *Designing a borrowing system*

Designing a borrowing system also requires careful organisation. The simplest method is the library lending book (Figure 14) in which a

Figure 14 The Library Lending Book

TITLE	BORROWER	borrowed	returned
The Kontiki Expedition	Bo Andersson	2/5	16/5
Man & Modern Science	Li Fu Zhang	4.5.	9.5.
The woman who disappeared	Eva Krantz	6/5	7/5
who did it first ?	Françoise Dubois	9/5	11/5
Tales from Arab History	Smail Bemmoussat	10.5	17.5
airport			

student writes name, title of book, date of borrowing and date of return in the columns provided. An alternative method is the library catalogue, consisting of a simple card index, which students can help to make (Figure 15). Its design and construction can be built into the activities of a lesson, each student writing several cards after the teacher's model. This provides valuable study skills work: for example, how to construct a card index, how to set out information clearly, and how to place items in alphabetical order. This work is useful in the student's general academic development.

Teachers will have their own ideas about how to set up the card index, but one simple way is to set out information about the book on the front of the card and ask the students to write their name and the dates of borrowing and return in columns on the back. The return date is important because it provides a check for the teacher on how quickly a student reads a book. A new card, with author and title printed across the top, can be provided as the original fills

Figure 15 The Library Catalogue: index card

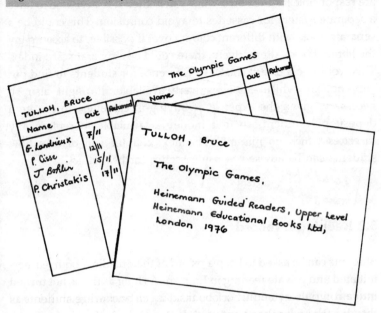

TULLOH, BRUCE

Name	out	Returned
G. Landrieux	7/11	
P. Cisse	12/11	
J Bohlin	15/11	
P. Christakis	17/11	

The Olympic Games

Name	out	Returned

TULLOH, Bruce

The Olympic Games,

Heinemann Guided Readers, Upper Level
Heinemann Educational Books Ltd,
London 1976

up. The added advantage of this method is that every time a student uses the index he is practising how to locate things in alphabetical order. The teacher, too, can make good use of the index since it will indicate clearly the types of book which are most popular. In the case of children, the use of a class library arranged in this manner, will encourage them to respect books and be interested in their care and use.

There is a growing number of cassettes now available to accompany graded Readers. Where financial resources are available, teachers may well be fortunate enough to have cassettes which students can borrow. In some institutions these might be housed with audio materials and students will borrow from a listening library or self study centre with its own cataloguing system. If teachers themselves are responsible for the borrowing system then it is advisable to have a separate system for cassettes to avoid confusion. This could be a separate book, with different colour cover if possible, to accompany the library book. Alternatively, there could be a separate card index. This would be a useful source of reference for students to find out very quickly which cassettes were available. It might also be necessary, given the expense of buying-in cassettes, to charge a deposit per student, so that money is available to replace any cassettes which go missing. The next chapter will discuss how students can be advised to use cassettes for best effect.

5.2 Keeping a record

Students can be asked to keep a record of their reading, both teacher-initiated and private reading in English. As long as this is not turned into a compulsory and laborious task, it can encourage students as they list the books they have read. It also gives the teacher a chance both to make a quick check on progress and to show a personal interest in students, attention which is usually appreciated.

5.2.1 Individual records

The record can take the form of a simple card, listing title and author (Figure 16), or a review notebook. (Figure 17)

With children in school, the personal record can be linked to art work in the curriculum. A long strip of coloured sugar paper or thin card, measuring 15cm by 60cm, can be folded to make a zig-zagged booklet of 15cm squares. On 12cm squares of white paper, younger children can draw a picture to represent the story they have read with a note of title and author and perhaps a few sentences in English about the book. Older children can write a short description of the

Figure 16 Examples of student record cards

DATE BORROWED	TITLE	DATE RETURNED
28 Sept 1984	Lucky Jim	5 Dec 1984
6 Dec 1984	Lucky Jim	12 Dec 1984
12 Dec 1984	the House on The Hill	19 Dec 1984
19 Dec 1984	Way Station	26 Dec 1984
28 Dec 1984	Madeleine	9 Jan 1985
9 Jan 1985	the Kraken Wakes	30 Jan 1985

DATE BORROWED	TITLE	DATE RETURNED
28 sept 1984	The Truth Machine	5 oct 1984
5 oct 1984	Last Tales	12 oct 1984
12 oct 1984	Winston Churchill	26 oct 1984
26 oct 1984	What's new	9 nov 1984
9 nov 1984	Tennis	16 nov 1984
16 nov 1984	Granny's first season	23 nov 1984
23 nov 1984	Islands	30 nov 1984
30 nov 1984	Elvis Presley	7 Dec 1984
7 dec 1984	Bristol Murder	14 dec 1984

Date Borrowed		Date returned
	A. Aziz AlSharif	
	33 Courtfield Gardens	
	Ealing – W-13	
	London	
16 –11–84	THE House oN the hill	
	Elizabeth Laird	
	the house on the hill	23 –11– 84
	Elizabeth Laird	
23-11-84	when the Drums beat and other	
	stories- Geoffrey trease	

story. These squares can be pasted into the booklet. The front page
of the booklet can record, in art form, how many books a child has
read, for example through adding spots to a ball, or cherries to a
bunch, or birds to a flock, whatever is culturally appropriate.

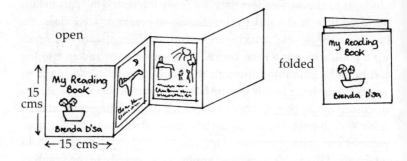

Figure 17 The individual reading record as art work

open

15 cms

←15 cms→

My Reading Book

Brenda D'sa

folded

My Reading Book

Brenda D'sa

5.2.2 *Class records*

As well as the children's personal records, some teachers like to display the reading progress of a class in some way, for example through a large wall chart. The chart can display a bar graph, listing students on the horizontal axis and marking number of books read on the vertical axis. Competitive displays like this might well be an incentive where motivation to read is low but it has to be remembered that there are possible disadvantages, too. It may be discouraging to slower readers and children may read hurriedly, without real understanding, in order to move up a step on the 'ladder' of the bar graph. Appendix III contains a note on the use of a chart in the Malaysian reading scheme.

Ideally the teacher should also keep a record for each student. This can be passed on to the teacher of the next class so that a student's progress is charted over a period of time. This record enables the teacher to check up on a student who seems not to be making good progress. It also provides information about an individual's interests and tastes so that future reading can be more usefully guided if necessary.

5.3 Directing and encouraging the choice of books

The most important thing here is that teachers should encourage students to choose Readers they are really interested in. This means allowing time in class, between classes, in breaks or after class, for browsing. Browsing, which can be fun, enables a student to pick up a book which interests him at a cursory glance and to use the technique of skimming through the book in order to decide if he wants to borrow it. In this way he is developing the kinds of strategies discussed in Chapter 4, those of previewing, predicting content from titles and chapter headings, getting ideas about the content from pictures and gaining an overall impression of a book. These are skills which good readers possess and apply unconsciously in their mother tongue, but they often seem to lack confidence in applying them to English books.

Sometimes students may ask the teacher's advice or the teacher may choose to guide students towards Readers related to their personal interests. If a student has read a book with evident enjoyment the teacher can suggest another with a similar topic or by the same author. If a student seems uninterested in reading, the teacher can try to discover interests to which a particular book might contribute. Or if a student chooses a book which is clearly too difficult, the teacher might guide him to a similar type of book at a lower level.

This is when it is important for the teacher to know both the books and the personal tastes and interests of students. It is all important that students are well motivated to read. Forcing students to read books with the mistaken idea that they are 'good for them' is a recipe for disaster. Even if some students never show an interest in 'good' classical or contemporary literature in an abridged or simplified form, then nothing is really lost. They are involved in reading something of interest to them, and through reading they are developing their knowledge of English. Haycraft (1979) makes a useful comment on this:

Don't confuse literary and language aims here. If your aim is linguistic don't insist that everything has literary value. Students will only read a lot if they are interested . . . so give them a book they don't want to put down.

5.4 Practical suggestions for promoting books

There are several other useful ways of encouraging reading and directing students to books.

(a) Students will often be encouraged to read a particular book by hearing an amusing, exciting or stimulating extract read dramatically by the teacher. Cassette recordings, with sound effects and the voices of professional actors, are particularly useful. They can add an extra dimension to the efforts of the classroom teacher and are especially valuable when the teacher is not a native speaker of English. Lively incidents from stories are usually successful or the first chapters of stories can whet the students' appetites, for example of *Arctic Oil Strike* ('Longman Structural Readers' 6) or *Interface* (Macmillan 'Rangers' Range 6).

(b) Sometimes students can be asked to give very short 'prepared' readings chosen from books they have enjoyed. The class can ask questions about the book after the reading. This activity develops students' confidence in producing English in front of an audience and contributes to general skills work by presenting the opportunity for controlled oral reading practice.

(c) As well as reading extracts, teachers can give recommendations explaining why they like certain books and what there is of interest in them. If a new book is added to the library, the teacher can give a brief review, pointing out what interest it may have for different groups of students.

(d) Student recommendations are even more successful. Students often like listening to each other saying how much they enjoyed certain books and they may well follow this kind of recommendation rather than the teacher's. Of course, students tell each other informally about good books. The message is passed on from one friend to another, and often results in a sudden 'rush' on a particular book, but it can be useful to formalise the passing on of tips as well. Students can be asked to prepare one minute talks, saying why they enjoyed a book and why they would recommend it, and a reading lesson can begin with these.

(e) Sometimes a topic in classwork may relate to the subject of a Reader and the teacher can mention it in passing. As shown in 4.3.3, a teacher using the same course book over a number of years can build up a list of Readers that relate to topics in the course book.

(f) Finally, as suggested in 5.1.2, any writing produced by students can also be displayed in the book corner to promote reading.

6 Individualised reading

6.1 Time for reading

Graded Readers can be used to 'fill gaps' in class time. Making sure that each student has a Reader ensures that he will have something to do when he is waiting for others to finish a particular task. This is one way of using Readers, especially useful where students are not able to take books home. And if a student is gripped by a book, the chance to read it in the spare moments of a lesson is a 'prize', an incentive to work well and quickly at other tasks.

Complementary to reading in class, where possible, is reading at home. This is the ideal alternative for part-time adult students in further education or private language schools, whose class time is limited.

Browsing in the book corner can be encouraged for a few minutes at the beginning of class while students are assembling or during the break where this is a normal part of the proceedings. But, for full-time students in school or adults following intensive courses, there are arguments in favour of establishing individual silent reading periods in class time, because this has a potential for self-directed learning that should not be ignored. After thorough preparation of the type suggested in Chapter 4, and with the kinds of self-access materials discussed later in this chapter, it can be a rewarding activity. Once a student has developed the habit of good and reasonably rapid reading in English, the opportunities for language learning out of class are considerable compared with the few hours of teacher controlled classwork per week.

6.2 Interviews

During the reading class the teacher can hold short, informal interviews with individual students about their reading. For some time, this has been established practice in mother-tongue teaching of English and in teaching English as a second language to young children. Teachers can try to arrange their classes in rooms which provide a quiet corner where these interviews can be conducted with least disturbance to the rest of the class. Books can be recommended and advice given about reading problems or useful activities for students to try.

The role of the teacher, then, is to advise, assist, remedy, widen the student's interests and encourage him to analyse his own reading experience by talking about the books he has read. For elementary students, interviews can be conducted in the first language but for students at higher levels this activity can provide an opportunity to speak English in real communicative situations. A teacher should have a mental checklist of possible points to cover in an interview, like the one in Figure 18, and choose items according to the particular needs of students.

Figure 18 Reader interview checklist

- check how many pages the student has read
- ask questions about the content or ask for a brief oral summary
- encourage the student to give some opinions on characters, events etc
- give help with any problems of comprehension (this is a good opportunity for individual help with dictionary skills or guessing meaning from textual clues)
- plan follow-up activities or check on those completed
- recommend further reading

6.3 Preparing for reading

Chapters 2 and 3 of this book placed emphasis on what the reader brings to a text. If a student reads in his mother tongue, he does so for a purpose, whether that purpose is idle curiosity about a subject or a deeper interest. But he brings ideas, feelings and opinions and a certain amount of knowledge to the reading of a book, which help to guide his understanding and which influence his reactions. People reading in a foreign language often need to be given support before they begin reading, an introduction which motivates reading by creating interest in the topic and which facilitates reading by developing background understanding and linguistic knowledge.

One way of preparing students individually for the books they are going to read is through the use of workcards. Given time, enthusiasm and a certain amount of expertise, a group of teachers can devise a simple workcard for each book in the library which provides context support and motivates reading. Figure 19 is a workcard showing how a student about to read *Visiting the USA* (Macmillan 'Rangers' Range 5) can try a quiz to see how much he already knows about the States. Reading the book will provide him with the opportunity to find information for the questions he couldn't answer.

Sometimes pictures from the graded Reader can be used to develop conceptual or language background. The story of *The Controllers* (Macmillan 'Rangers' Range 5) is one of a family going pot-holing and the adventures they meet with underground. Many students will be unfamiliar with this pastime but an easy way to introduce some of the new terms is to exploit the picture in the way suggested on the workcard (Figure 20).

The idea of developing a set of workcards is an ambitious one and the task itself is very demanding on teachers. It may take several years to build up a full set but, once the task is begun, workcards provide valuable opportunities for individualising reading and all sorts of other related activities which create confidence and pleasure.

Figure 19

How much do you know about the USA?
Before you read the book, see how many of these questions you
can answer.
When you read the book you will find the answers.

1 What is the capital of the USA?
2 Where does the President of the USA live?
3 Which were the last two states to join the USA?
4 What do Americans call a taxi?
5 What are these: a Greyhound Station?
                   an automat?
                   a subway?
                   a reservation?
6 Who or what is 'Old Faithful'?
7 Can you name three American coins?
8 Where is Disneyland?
9 Which language, not English, can you hear a lot of people
   talk in Los Angeles?
10 Why is it easy to find your way in New York?
11 Which of these can you find in New York?
    a) Statue of Liberty   b) Pentagon
    c) St Patrick's Cathedral   d) United Nations
15 Beverley Hills, Malibou, Hollywood and Santa Monica are
    all parts of the same city. Which city is it?
16 What happened in San Francisco on April 18th, 1906?
17 What are the roads in Los Angeles called?
18 When is Independence Day?

Workcard for VISITING THE USA by Georgiana
Melrose (Macmillan 'Rangers' Range 5)

Figure 20

Muff, Roy and their father go pot-holing one weekend and meet with some exciting adventures. Pot-holing is a sport for people who like climbing down deep holes in the ground. They enjoy exploring subterranean caves, rivers and lakes. Would you like to go pot-holing? What sort of person would you have to be? What would it be like? How would you feel?

Answer these questions. Make a list of English words you know.

What sort of person would you have to be? . . . careful? . . .
What would it be like? . . . dangerous? . . .
How would you feel? . . . afraid? . . .

The children and their father have to take special equipment with them. Look at the picture. What is each piece of equipment for? Match the names with the explanations. You will find the correct answers when you read the book.

to hammer pegs in the rock

f) sleeping bags

to keep you warm when you sleep

b) helmets

to help you see in the dark

a) rope ladders

to climb down deep chimneys

e) flashlights

to help you swim underwater

c) wet suits

g) hammers

to keep you warm in cold water

to protect your head if you fall

d) aqualungs

They spent the rest of the day planning the descent and checking their equipment.

Workcard for THE CONTROLLERS by Peter
Keane (Macmillan 'Rangers' Range 5)

6.4 Using cassettes for individualised reading

Many cassettes are now available from publishers to accompany graded Readers. Cassettes can be useful aids to students reading at home. The dramatisation of a story with different voices and sound effects or an expressive narration can assist comprehension considerably. Teachers can suggest various methods of using a cassette and should advise students to vary these so that their motivation is sustained (Figure 21).

Figure 21 Advice on using a Reader Cassette

(a) Decide on a part of the story you are going to listen to and mark it. Play the cassette while you are reading. Don't stop the cassette until you come to the place you have marked to finish. Try to understand as much as possible. After you have stopped the cassette, go back and check words and sentences you were uncertain about.

(b) Give yourself a listening exercise sometimes and just listen before reading. It will help to give you a general idea of the story before you start to read.

(c) Read part of the story before you listen. Don't stop to look up unknown words but try to understand the main points. Then play the cassette to see if the dramatisation, sound effects or narrator's voice help you to understand better.

(d) Occasionally you could try reading aloud with the cassette, but don't do this too often because you usually read more slowly when you read aloud and you may slow down your silent reading speed.

When students use cassettes for the first time, it is worth taking ten minutes with the class to outline these methods. Alternatively, points (a) to (d) above can be written on a poster to be displayed in the book corner or duplicated on a stencil and handed out to students.

Cassettes are also an invaluable aid in class and their use in classwork is discussed in section 7.1.6.

6.5 Individualising activities

The initial aim of silent reading time in class or private reading at home is to provide conditions for the effort and concentration demanded by reading a foreign language. The ultimate aim is to make reading enjoyable. This means that the focus should always be on reading as an end in itself. Some students take great pleasure in doing various kinds of follow-up activity, but others, who enjoy the reading itself, may think nothing more boring than producing 'work', an anticipated task which takes away motivation and detracts from the primary pleasure of reading. It is therefore important to allow for individual tastes and if a pupil prefers to spend all his time reading, then perhaps he should be encouraged simply to read.

Other students enjoy and see the value in activities associated with their reading which enable them to develop related language skills, and will work happily on individual assignments suggested by the teacher. Here are some of the general activities that individual students often enjoy and that teachers can try with students at an appropriate level.

6.5.1 *Keeping a book diary*

This appeals to many students. With students at lower levels of language competence, a book record of the kind discussed in 5.2.1 is an embryonic diary. Students able to write more in English can decide what to include, whether it should be a simple notation of author and title or whether it should describe characters, events, or even excerpts from favourite passages. The diary should be quite separate from the topic vocabulary book suggested in 4.2.2. Its purpose should be to use language to write about the content of the book.

Figure 22

WRITING A BOOK REVIEW

TITLE: What is the title of the book?

AUTHOR: Who wrote it?

TYPE: Is it a detective story, spy thriller, horror story, historical novel, science fiction, romance, etc.?

SUBJECT: What is it about. e.g. family life, an unusual person, a mystery, an adventure?

CHARACTERS: Who are they? What are they like?

SETTING: Where does the story take place?

TIME: Is it written in the present time, or is it historical, or set in the future?

EVENTS: What happens? (Don't tell the whole story, just enough to interest your readers)

IDEAS: Is the writer saying something important about people? Is there a 'message' in the story?

COMMENTS: What was it like to read? easy/difficult?
                                        short/long?

              How would you describe the story?
                                        realistic? amusing?
                                        exciting? thrilling?
                                        fast-moving? sad?

              Did you like it?
              What did you like especially about it?
              How did you feel? happy? sad?

Figure 23

BOOK REVIEW
WORKSHEET (Reviewing)

Write a *review* of a book that you have finished.

To help you, first complete these *notes* about your book.

A *Basic facts about the book*

    1 Title
    2 Author
    3 Publisher
    4 Date of publication
    5 ISBN number
    6 (Price)

B *Type of book*

    1 Fiction/non-fiction
    2 Long/short
      a) no. of pages
      b) no. of words (guess)
    3 illustrated/not illustrated
      a) photographs
      b) drawings
      c) other

C *Content* MAKE NOTES ONLY!

    1 *Fiction*
      a) Story when
               where
               brief summary
      b) Characters how many
                   names
                   relationships

2 *Non-fiction*
   a) subject/topic general
                  specific
   b) chapters/sections how many
                      topics

D *Reactions* TRY TO GIVE REASONS!
   1 (too) easy/(too) difficult
   2 like/dislike
   3 interesting/boring

E *Conclusions*
   1 When did you read the book?
   2 How long did it take to read it?
   3 Would you like another book by the same author/on the same subject/ of the same type?
   4 Would you recommend it to anyone?

NOW USE YOUR NOTES TO HELP YOU WRITE YOUR BOOK REVIEW. YOUR TEACHER WILL HELP YOU MAKE THE RIGHT SORTS OF SENTENCES

Good Luck!   Norman Whitney

6.5.2 *Writing reviews*

The teacher can provide models for this activity by reviewing a couple of books from the collection and displaying the reviews so that they are accessible to students. Students' own reviews can similarly be displayed to interest and encourage their classmates. Alternatively, or in addition, the teacher can display a 'guide' with a series of questions around which students can frame their own reviews. An example of a guide for intermediate students is given in Figure 22. This can be introduced and explained in class time. During individual interviews in class reading time, the teacher can help students to formulate and organise their ideas about books and can assist with review writing. A worksheet of the kind shown in Figure 23 can be used to help students to prepare their reviews.

6.5.3 *Describing a character*

A common item in an English course is the lesson on 'describing people', learning the vocabulary to describe appearance, dress, personality, and character. Asking students to describe a favourite, interesting, or unusual character from their Reader is good language practice and a useful way of exploiting a Reader more intensively for vocabulary work and the organisation of descriptive writing.

6.5.4 *Designing a book cover*

Students can design the cover for a new edition of the book to include comments from reviewers in the manner of a typical paperback, such as:

'A powerful and exciting story . . .'

'Fast-moving and full of suspense . . .'

'Very good entertainment . . .'

— and a summary of the contents for the inside cover. If this work can be integrated with other curriculum subjects such as art and design, it will add to the pleasure of the activity.

6.5.5 *Writing a letter to the author*

This activity has the advantage of being real and may even elicit a reply if sent to the publisher. Students can practise letter writing by formulating a letter to the author with appreciative comments, questions and criticisms about the book.

6.5.6 *Interviewing a character*

Some books provide interesting characters such as great inventors, famous scientists, film actors and statesmen, with whom students could conduct 'imaginary interviews', and the interview could be presented in the form of a written script. This form of article is popular in English magazines nowadays. Thinking up questions to ask these famous people and finding information from the book for answers or speculating on imaginary answers is creative language work for students, which practises reading and writing skills in a usefully integrated way.

6.5.7 *Researching a topic*

Sometimes a book suggests an area of research around a topic. For example, a book of biographies like *Five Famous Inventors* or *Six Great Scientists* or *Great People of our Time* (Macmillan 'Rangers' Range 6) can stimulate 'research' on famous figures from the students' own culture. A book of folktales like *Princess Moonlight* (Macmillan 'Rangers' Range 5) may interest students in finding folk tales from their own tradition.

It is useful for students to research in their mother tongue but to present their findings in English. In this way foreign language learning activities can contribute to the general development of study skills in the curriculum.

6.5.8 *Individual workcards*

Apart from these general ideas, individual books will present their own possibilities for follow-up work. Figure 24, which is the back of the workcard for *Visiting the USA* (see Figure 19), shows how activities can be devised which are appropriate to the topic of a particular Reader.

Figure 24 Workcard for VISITING THE USA (Cont'd)

ACTIVITIES

1 Imagine you are going to visit the USA. Where would you go and what would you do?

   a) Draw a map (use the one at the beginning of the book) and mark your route.

   b) Write a composition saying where you want to visit, and why, and what you would do there.

2 Use your book to find information and make notes about these things:
   — the weather   — travel
   — where to stay   — sightseeing
   — what to eat

   Now make an 'information brochure' for tourists who are going to the USA.

3 Which of these towns would you most like to visit?
   New York Chicago Washington DC Los Angeles San Francisco

   Make notes about the town under these headings:

Where?	How big?	Why famous?	Where to go?	What to do?

Use your notes to write a short description of the town.

These suggestions for follow up activities are intended to motivate reading and develop related language skills but they should always be regarded as secondary to the primary aim of encouraging the process of reading itself.

7 Using a class Reader

The choice of a class Reader needs to be made carefully, with reference to the criteria discussed in Chapter 3. It is perhaps too ambitious to hope that any one Reader will suit every student in the class, but the subject matter needs to motivate the majority; otherwise it will hardly develop their interest in reading.

The organisation of class reading also requires careful handling. The traditional method is to go through the book in class, with the teacher reading aloud or students reading 'around the class' for one lesson a week. The problems with this method, where everyone is obliged to read at the same pace, is that the quicker or more interested students skip on quickly through the book. A much more successful approach is to set most of the reading for homework or to allow students to read at their own pace during class time. The greater proportion of class time can then be spent on checking reading, working with key passages, class discussion and various follow-up activities.

7.1 Starting a new Reader

There are several ways in which a teacher can promote interest in a new book and, at the same time, develop background understanding and relevant language knowledge.

(a) The workcards shown in Chapter 6 are as useful for classwork as for individualised reading. For example, the card on *Visiting the USA* (Figure 19) can be used as a competitive game. Questions can be put on the blackboard, a poster or an overhead transparency before the lesson, a class of twenty students can be divided into groups of four and each group can work out answers as quickly as possible. The card on *The Controllers* (Figure 20) can be used for class discussion: the teacher can explain a little about pot-holing (pictures of underground caves would be useful) and can then elicit vocabulary from the class by using the questions on the card:

What sort of person would you have to be? . . . strong, brave . . .
What would it be like? . . . dangerous, cold, dark, wet . . .

Workcards like these introduce the stories in different ways, by giving a brief outline of when and where events occur and what characters are involved, by introducing the topic of the story and key words related to it.

(b) Using illustrations is another way of creating interest in a Reader and establishing background knowledge. For example, *A River Ran Out of Eden* by James Vance Marshall ('Heinemann Guided Readers' Elementary) is set on the Aleutian Islands and the story relates to the animal life. If the teacher can collect maps, pictures and photographs to give an impression of the setting and the animal life, and paste them on to a large wall chart, this is very motivating preparation. The teacher can talk a little about the various items on the wall chart and elicit what students might already know about this part of the world.

(c) Sometimes a non-fiction book can be introduced by setting up a class activity around an extract from the book. *A Woman's Place?* by Monica Vincent ('Longman Structural Readers' Stage 4) contains a questionnaire 'How Equal is Your Marriage?' which can be used for pair work practice and discussion. It also has a specimen contract between husband and wife about roles and responsibilities in the household, *The ACE Family Contract*, and this has been used successfully with advanced classes of mixed adults as a basis for group and whole-class discussion. Both of these activities form a natural way in to the topic of the book.

(d) A dramatic reading of the first chapter or first section of a book can provide enjoyment and motivation and, at the same time, can integrate extensive reading usefully with extensive listening. This reading can be purely for enjoyment with some general questions afterwards and an elicitation from students of what they think might happen next. Or it can be introduced with some pre-listening questions formulated so that students pick out the most important points for their understanding of the story. Questions could require brief note-taking, another useful skill. *Dangerous Game* ('Longman Structural Readers' 3), *Outcast* ('Alpha Historical Fiction', OUP) and *The Kraken Wakes* ('Longman Simplified English Series') are examples of books with intriguing first chapters which lend themselves to this (Figure 25). Alternatively a reading of the first story in a book of short stories such as *Me, Myself and I* ('Longman Structural Readers' 4) can whet the appetite.

Figure 25 Examples of pre-listening questions for *Dangerous Game*

```
What is the name of the main character?
What does he do?
What kind of house does he live in?
How old is he?
How long has his wife been dead?
Who is Louis?
Why does he visit the house?
Who is Poldy?
```

(e) For the teacher with access to a cassette recorder, a cassette can be used for listening to an extract from the book. Cassettes add much to the enjoyment of a story. They are an invaluable aid to the non-native speaker teachers who want their students to hear mother-tongue English speakers. They present a range of accents and create a lively atmosphere. Most of all, they can be played back for repeat performances of difficult bits of text. This last facility means that students can listen once to see how well they understand and then listen again with some kind of while-listening task. *Women in Britain* by Catherine Wallace ('Evans Graded Reading' Grade 4) lends itself well to this because it has seven self contained articles about different women. Students could listen to the extract on Kuljit, an Indian woman in Britain, and do the true/false activity in Figure 26.

Figure 26 A true/false exercise

Tick the true statements.

Kuljit says:
- [ ] she didn't find it hard to adjust to life in Britain.
- [ ] she prefers to wear an Indian sari.
- [ ] her family respected her wish to complete her education.
- [ ] Indian women are expected to be obedient.
- [ ] her family were disappointed when she refused an offer of marriage.
- [ ] an Indian woman requires a good education to take up a career.
- [ ] she agrees with the Women's Liberation Movement.
- [ ] she thinks men and women should have more equal roles in marriage.

7.2 Methods of reading the book

At the beginning of this chapter mention was made of how best to deal with a class Reader, setting some reading for homework and doing some in class. Reading in class can be of several types.

(a) If a teacher wants to promote silent reading in the classroom, either to encourage the habit of extensive reading or possibly because students are not permitted to take Readers home, it is possible to let students read at their own pace with the teacher checking individually for comprehension, for example by going through questions or points for understanding chapter by chapter.

(b) Probably the most traditional way of reading the book is for the teacher to read (or the cassette as storyteller to dramatise) while students listen and follow in their books. The teacher needs to decide on the length of any uninterrupted stretches of listening/reading and to be prepared at the end of each stretch to deal with any of the following: clarifying difficult vocabulary or idioms; explaining problems in understanding cultural information; checking comprehension by asking questions or preparing worksheets. Many graded Readers contain glossaries, lists of new words, idioms, exercises in comprehension and structure, chapter by chapter questions to focus on important points for understanding, questions for pair work and questions for class discussion. Students can be directed to whichever of these are useful and relevant and teachers can exploit many of the exercises for class activity.

(c) Group reading can be used with dramatic scripts. Again, the teacher must decide how long a piece of script to prepare. The teacher can read first to produce a model and provide any necessary support to understanding, then let students read individual speeches round the class for practice before allocating parts to small groups of students who will try to read dramatically. Teachers who have tried this will know that it rarely produces perfect dramatic reading but it does provide fun and motivation. Recording the group efforts on tape and playing them back is also amusing and gives learners a sense of their own progress and areas for improvement.

Cassettes are particularly effective for this kind of activity, both with dramatic scripts and with stories where there is a good deal of conversation. Students can be prepared by listening to the cassette first and following in their books. Then the teacher can allot parts. As the cassette is played a second time, the teacher can stop it whenever a character starts speaking so that a student can read the part instead. Then the recording can continue so that the class can compare the student's performance with the 'real thing'. In this way, the recording tells the story and the students participate to improve their pronunciation.

(d) A great deal has been written in recent years about the inadvisability of reading out loud in the classroom. There are undoubtedly reasons to justify this doubt. However, oral reading has several points in its favour if seen as one possible activity in a range and not as the sole method of reading. Figure 27 is a checklist of points for and against oral reading.

Figure 27 Points for and against oral reading

For
- students often read out loud as an aid to making sense of sentences and finding the boundaries of sense groups
- it gives extra practice in pronunciation, word stress and rhythm
- it brings variety to classroom activities
- it is appropriate to certain kinds of texts such as poetry and drama
- many students enjoy oral reading and are motivated by it
- traditionally it is the mode of reading in many educational systems

Against
- listening to inaccurate pronunciation from classmates confuses understanding of the sound-symbol relationship
- the reader is so intent on articulation that he loses track of the content
- it does not allow the reader to use natural strategies for reading quickly and forces him to revert to a slow reading of every word so that overall meaning may be lost through attention to detail
- it requires a considerable amount of class time that might be better exploited

The fact is that reading aloud exists as a standard procedure in English Language teaching throughout the world, and the sensible line to take is therefore how to make it most effective. As Alun L W Rees states, in a usefully detailed paper on the subject (1980:112-121):

> Reading aloud by the learner from the class text is such a seemingly straightforward and inevitable use of the printed page that it continually re-occurs in language teaching and will undoubtedly go on doing so, despite repeated doses of potent theoretical purgatives. A diagnosis of 'allowed' or 'not allowed' is therefore somewhat superfluous: what we need is the remedy for improving the state of this chronic and frequently ill-treated technique.

Passages for reading aloud from the chapter of the book can be allocated to students for homework. This allows for preparation time and means that the teacher can allocate more difficult passages to better students and vice versa. The ideal is to type the passages adding stress marks, indicating sense groups in some way and possibly even intonation. Teachers can decide on their own system, to suit themselves and their students. Figure 28 uses:

- separate lines to show sense groups and pauses
- dots to mark stress
- capitals to mark words which should be given special emphasis

Figure 28 An example of annotation for reading aloud

One day,

at noon,

Ivor walked into the local pub,

The Horse and Dragon,

looking VERY worried.

Intonation marks for fall \ and rise / could be added too.

The passages can be pasted on to card to preserve them and the cards numbered in the order in which passages occur in the chapter. If a chapter of an intermediate Reader breaks down into six passages of 100 words each, then the class can be divided into groups of six students. Each student in the class prepares his passage at home and then will work in his group, each student reading the cards in order, helping each other and monitored by the teacher. Six students can then be asked to read the chapter while the rest of the class listens. It is an effective technique and well worth trying.

7.3 Planning a scheme of work for a Reader

The teacher should plan a programme in advance for dealing with a graded Reader. This will ensure a good range of reading methods and a variety of follow up work in the classroom. Figure 29 is a model scheme of work for reading *Johnny Ring* (Macmillan 'Rangers' Range 4) for which a cassette is available. Six lessons of 45 minutes each every week would provide a half term's work.

Figure 29 Programme for *Johnny Ring*
            (Macmillan 'Rangers' Range 4)

Lesson 1	Introduction and warm up — use map in book to set scene — elicit what Ss know about civil war — use texts p10, p16 for intensive reading Listen to beginning of story Set reading at home pps 1-7
Lesson 2	Play cassette pps 1-7 — deal with problems and ask general questions — key vocabulary exercise on worksheet Set pps 8-16 for reading at home Ask Ss to make 5 questions about passage.

Lesson 3	Pair work questions on pps 8-16 Use pictures on worksheets for oral summary work. Play pps 17-19 in class with pre-listening questions Use text p 18 *The Civil War* for intensive reading Set pps 19-22 to prepare for oral reading.
Lesson 4	Oral reading in groups Follow up work on vocabulary Use inset text p20 *'The Union and the Confederacy'* for intensive reading Set pp 22-27 for homework with questions
Lesson 5	Listen to pages 19-27 on cassette. Deal with vocabulary, use set questions Follow up on language — an events ordering exercise — an exercise on verbs Set pps 27-39 for HW — Ss to make question
Lesson 6	Pair work question and answer Take points pp 27-39 with general questions Use cassette for listening while reading of final dramatic pages. Discussion of Ss response to book. Set an assortment of writing tasks eg. review, summary, project etc.

This scheme shows a suggested structure for one class as follows:
1 Recapping and checking of the pages set for homework by questioning of various types.
2 Follow up work of various kinds
     eg intensive reading
          using pictures
          oral summary
          key vocabulary work
3   Key passages for intensive classwork with explanation and discussion

eg listening to a cassette
   dramatic reading by the teacher
   oral reading in groups
4 Set reading for following week with
   either questions set by teacher to guide reading
   or students to read and devise questions about the reading.

The activities within any lesson should be varied and will focus on general comprehension and interpretation of the text but can also contain useful language work deriving from the book. Some ideas for language activities are suggested in 7.4 below.

7.4 Asking questions about books

There are three principles worth bearing in mind when formulating questions to guide students as they read chapters at home or to ask students when recapping, or when dealing with a key passage in class.

(a) The first is quite simply that **questions should be relevant to the students' age and language level.** *Johnny Ring* on one level is an exciting adventure story and for younger readers the story itself and how they react to characters and events may be sufficient focus. For older readers questions may well venture (remembering that this is only Range 4) into their reactions to slavery, war, self sacrifice and heroism. In terms of language competence the questions (and the anticipated responses they provoke) must be within the appropriate language range.

(b) The second is that **students, as well as teachers, can ask questions.** Instead of giving students questions to answer while reading at home, the teacher can ask students to prepare questions to ask their classmates. This involves students in reviewing what they have read and making sense of it sufficiently to formulate sensible questions. While listening to the pair work arising from this or to the class question-answer session, the teacher can judge how successfully students have read.

(c) **The focus of questions should be on comprehension, evaluation, and response to reading** rather than details of the language. Questions can therefore concentrate on

- the characters, events and actions of the book
- how students respond to these.

Here is a selection of these two types of questions from a discussion of *Johnny Ring*, pps 24-31.

- Why did Johnny rush back across the bridge?
  How did Johnny feel as he struggled across the bridge?
  Why did the soldiers cheer?
  Why couldn't the Captain get back to the camp?

- Why do you think the sword was so important to Johnny?
  Do you think he was brave?
  Do you think the Captain was wrong to leave the camp?

The main point to remember is that the purpose of questions should not only be to assist understanding but also to encourage students to respond and reflect so that reading becomes an enjoyable educational experience.

8 Using Readers as an extra classroom resource

Readers can be a useful classroom resource, particularly useful to teachers working in situations where resources are meagre. A set of class Readers, even when shared one between two students, can be exploited for many kinds of more intensive classroom work.

There is an increasing amount of commercially-produced material available to accompany Readers or to accompany cassettes. For example, Longman produce sets of exercises to accompany cassettes. These exercises are of various kinds, including:

- sentences describing events in the story with blanks to be filled in
- sets of questions which can be used for oral work in class
- comprehension checks of various kinds
- activities to develop summary writing skills

Macmillan produce 'kits' to go with their 'Ranger' Readers. A Ranger Reading Kit will contain Readers, cassettes, dictionaries, wall-posters and Activity Books containing games, comprehension work, puzzles, vocabulary exercises and writing activities in relation to each book.

However, there are many activities of a home-made kind which teachers can devise both for language study and for the development of language skills in various ways and combinations.

8.1 Readers as a resource for language study

Graded Readers can be exploited for various types of language study in class. Many of these activities would derive from more intensive reading of parts of the book and, as such, do not really fall within the scope of a book on extensive reading. Another book in this series (Williams: 1984) looks at intensive reading in the classroom and related activities and contains many useful suggestions for more intensive language work.

However, it seems appropriate and useful to conclude this book on graded Readers with a list of ideas and suggestions for activities which teachers can devise for their own students. Examples 19-28 and 30-31 are all taken from the Activity Books which accompany Macmillan's 'Ranger' Readers. They show how exercises and puzzles of this kind can be used for the study of vocabulary, structure and textual cohesion.

8.1.1 Vocabulary study

Graded Readers are clearly a means of developing and expanding vocabulary and can be exploited for word building activities and exercises. Example 19 demonstrates how the meaning of adjectives can be made clear through using the context of the story. Both Examples 19 and 20 use the traditional blank filling technique to pick out and practise certain parts of speech. In Example 21 new vocabulary from the story is highlighted and used to develop an 'opposites' exercise. Example 22, 'Working with Words', encourages students to use their dictionaries so that teachers have the opportunity to monitor and assist the development of good dictionary skills such as locating words in alphabetical order. Learners can arrange their own lists in alphabetical order as a consolidation exercise. Word puzzles, as in Example 23, are always popular with students. This particular example is appropriate to young learners, while more sophisticated crosswords can be designed for older students.

Example 19

How do they feel?

Look at what these people say. Can you tell how they feel?
Look at the words below and choose one for each person.
Write the word at the side.

1 *Maggi:* Please come with me to the hills. I don't want to go alone.

                                        _____

2 *Thomas:* I have a lot of things to do.

                                        _____

3 *Thomas:* You're a bad girl. You bring me all this way up the hill and there is
nothing here.

                                        _____

4 *Dr Aziz:* Thank you, Maggi, for all your help. You are helping us all.

                                        _____

5 *Father:* Is this another one of your stories, Maggi?

                                        _____

6 *Man:* My mother is ill. Now I can buy something to make her well.

                                        _____

angry	happy	unhappy
busy	afraid	thankful

Activity Book for *Maggi and the UFO* p11,
Beatrice Conway (Macmillan 'Rangers' Range 1)

Example 20

Where?

**Put the right word in these sentences. Number 8 is *through*.
You can see that from the picture. Now you do these.**

up   through   in   from   to   with   on   by

1   Tom works _____ Sam's shop.

2   It is a big town _____ the sea.

3   The ships come _____ different countries.

4   The ship is going _____ America.

5   The top of the mast is a long way _____ .

6   Where is that small boy _____ the big knife?

7   Something falls _____ Tom's head.

8   Some men are coming *through* the water.

Activity Book for *Cash on the Nail* p4, Gillian
Armstrong (Macmillan 'Rangers' Range 1)

Example 21

Opposites

Write down the word which means the opposite in these sentences.

1 Ted isn't *good-looking*. He's _____.

2 First, *open* the door. Then _____ it.

3 That is the *wrong* road. Do you know the _____ one?

4 One man can *push* and the other can _____ .

5 This place isn't *safe*. It's _____ .

6 The boat isn't *empty*. It's _____ .

7 The work isn't *easy*. It's _____ .

8 The boat *arrives* at the Falls in the morning and it _____ in the evening.

9 The music is *soft*. It isn't _____ .

Activity Book for *Up the Creek* p4, Paul Aston
(Macmillan 'Rangers' Range 2)

Example 22

Working with words

Everyone has his favourite food. Griselda likes
bananas and coffee. The lions like meat. What's
your favourite food? The following list of words is
from your book, *A Learner's First Dictionary*. If
there are any words that you don't understand,
look them up. Arrange the words in alphabetical
order.

rice   beans   tea   ice-cream   apples   eggs

cheese   strawberries   coffee   potatoes   bread

corn   cake   nuts   oranges   chicken   milk

beef   pears   fish

Now make a list of your ten favourite things to eat
and a list of ten things that you don't like to eat at
all. Are there some things on your lists that do not
appear among the words above? What are they?

Food that I like   **Food that I don't like**

_____   _____

_____   _____

_____   _____

_____   _____

_____   _____

_____   _____

_____   _____

_____   _____

Look at your classmate's list. Is it the same?

Activity Book for *The Ghost of Beestley Zoo* p 5,
St James (Macmillan 'Rangers' Range 2)

Example 23

Looking for words

How many words can you find in the UFO? They are
words from the story which tell you what people do.
Maggi is a shepherd girl. There are four more words. Can
you find them? You can read across or down.

Write the words here.

1 _____

2 _____

3 _____

4 _____

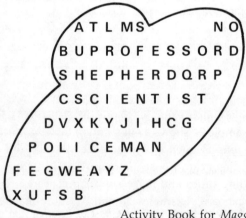

Activity Book for *Maggi and the UFO*, p11,
Beatrice Conway (Macmillan 'Rangers' Range 1)

Sometimes it is possible to use a character from the Reader and develop vocabulary for describing people. This activity was suggested in Chapter 6 for individualised work but it is also an excellent opportunity for all students to participate in class work. The teacher can elicit from students what they can remember about the character and build up information on the blackboard in columns like this:

Appearance	Dress	Personality	Your Opinions

For the last column the teacher can present simple ways of evaluating people. For example:

I think he is a kind and sympathetic person.
I don't like this person. He is too ambitious.

8.1.2 *Structure study*

Teachers can also make simple exercises to practise structures taken from the Reader. Example 24 shows a substitution table to practise the word order and tense sequence of a sentence like *I will call you when I am ready*. Teachers can choose a structure which is new to the level of the reading series and make similar practice exercises to write on the blackboard. Examples 30 and 31 show matching exercises which test the students' comprehension of the story but also, implicitly, practise a structure.

Example 24

Making sentences

Write ten sentences using words from below.
Choose one word from each of A, B, C, D, E, F, G,
and H.

Example: I will call you when I am ready.

A	B	C	D
I	will	call	you
you	can	wait for	me
Karen	has to	help	him
Tom	have to		go
They			her
			them

E	F	G	H
although	I	are	tired
when	he	is	ready
until	the work	am	busy
as soon as	you	have	here
	they		finished
	the taxi		

Activity Book for *Every Dog has his Day* p8, Gillian
Armstrong (Macmillan 'Rangers' Range 2)

Example 25

Why ?. . . because. . .

**Which is the right answer to these questions? Put the letter
of the answer in the box next to the question number.**

1 ☐ Why can't Kansky land?

2 ☐ Why can't Dr James leave the hospital?

3 ☐ Why is Dr Armstrong very tired?

4 ☐ Why does Lancing want to make a fire?

5 ☐ Why doesn't the pilot want to fly round
looking for them?

a He is low on petrol.

b There are too many trees.

c He wants to cook dinner.

d He has too much petrol.

e He hasn't slept in 34 hours.

f He has worked for 22 hours.

g He wants to keep warm.

h One of his patients is ill.

Activity Book for *Flying Doctor* p11, Alwyn Cox
(Macmillan 'Rangers' Range 2)

Example 26

Finish the sentences

**Choose the right sentence from B and add it to
the sentence in A to make one long sentence.
Write them below.**

A

1   If Steve works late

2   If nobody comes for the dogs

3   If Mary takes Fred to the shop

4   If the police get a piece of cloth

5   If Mary starts work

6   If the editor is thankful

B

a   he'll give Fred a present.

b   she'll work at home.

c   Mary will be all alone.

d   she'll be ill.

e   Mrs King will help.

f   they can prove who the burglar
    is.

g   they will give them away.

h   some customers will not like it.

Activity Book for *Every Dog has his Day* p9,
Gillian Armstrong (Macmillan 'Rangers' Range 2)

Another type of exercise can be devised to practise sentence structure. In Example 27 students have to sort out the jumbled sentences and, in doing so, their understanding of word order in simple sentences can be developed.

Example 27

What are they saying?

What are these people from the story saying?
Move the words round to make sentences.

Activity Book for *Up the Creek* p1, Paul Aston
(Macmillan 'Rangers' Range 2)

8.1.3 *Textual study*

More intensive reading of parts of the text can give rise to textual study. For example, an events-ordering exercise, as in Example 28, practises understanding of the cohesive features in text, how words like 'it' and 'he' and 'them' structure a text.

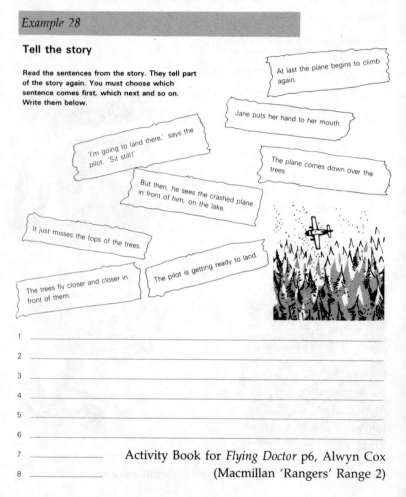

Example 28

Tell the story

Read the sentences from the story. They tell part of the story again. You must choose which sentence comes first, which next and so on. Write them below.

At last the plane begins to climb again.

Jane puts her hand to her mouth.

'I'm going to land there,' says the pilot. 'Sit still!'

The plane comes down over the trees.

But then, he sees the crashed plane in front of him, on the lake.

It just misses the tops of the trees.

The trees fly closer and closer in front of them.

The pilot is getting ready to land.

1 _____
2 _____
3 _____
4 _____
5 _____
6 _____
7 _____   Activity Book for *Flying Doctor* p6, Alwyn Cox
8 _____   (Macmillan 'Rangers' Range 2)

8.2 Readers as a resource for skills work

Reading is not the only skill that can be practised with graded Readers. Much can be gained by integrating reading with listening, speaking or writing.

8.2.1 *Listening practice*

Short passages from Readers can be used for listening practice. This is particularly good where a cassette is available but the teacher can read aloud to good effect as well. Example 29 is a reasonably self contained extract. Even so, the teacher should begin by 'warming up' to the listening task. Here are suggested steps for the activity:

1 Teacher asks questions to warm up to the story, eg
  Do you ever walk home in the dark?
  Is it a good idea to walk alone?
  What can happen?
  What happens to John in this story?
2 Let students listen once to the story and ask them for answers to the last question.
3 Give the students a listening task, for example true/false statements (Figure 30) to listen for during the second listening.

Figure 30 A true/false exercise

	Tick (✔)	True	False
John usually went home by bus.			
He turned left from the street into a dark alley.			
John was short and thin.			
Three men stepped into his path.			

4 Teacher and students check through the answers together.

Example 29

John's home was only half a mile away and he usually walked home in the evening. He did so tonight, even though a bus came along that would have stopped near the red-brick house where he lived with his mother.

John put up the collar of his coat and walked quickly down the street. At the bottom of the hill he turned left, as usual, to go down a long dark alley. It was shorter than going along the street.

Half way down the alley two figures stepped out of the shadows and blocked his way. John suddenly felt frightened. He was not big and strong like the two men who now stood opposite him. He was tall but rather thin.

The larger of the two men, and the older of the two, spoke first: 'Are you Farthing?'

'Yes. Who are you?' John sounded very nervous.

'We've a message for you,' replied the man, with a nasty look on his face.

'Oh?' said John.

'Stop making a nuisance of yourself if you want to stay pretty.' The message was delivered to John in a quiet, threatening voice.

John looked behind him, ready to run for it, but both men seized him by the arms. John struggled to free himself.

'What do you think you're doing?' he demanded.

'It's for your own good, my lad,' said the other man. 'We're just giving you a warning.'

'What have I done to you?'

'You're making stupid phone calls about the past,' said the man, twisting his arm behind his back, 'so forget it, or else . . . !'

The bigger man then hit him hard in the stomach. John could not resist. He doubled up and fell to the ground. The other man kicked him in the back. Then the two men ran off, leaving him moaning and breathless.

John lay still for a few minutes, trying to get his breath back. His body ached all over. The pain in his back was terrible, and he had a nasty lump on his head. He could hardly move. No one seemed to be around so his cry for help went unanswered.

At last he picked himself up, swearing at the pain it caused him, and started to walk down the alley. He arrived home ten minutes later. His face was so pale and his coat so dirty and wet, it gave his mother a shock to see him. He was in such a bad state that she phoned for a doctor immediately.

John did not dare tell his mother about the men who had beaten him up. She would ask questions and want to call the police. And he didn't want to talk to the police. He could not tell them about the warning the two men had given him. How could he accuse George Crombie and David Pilger of anything? Both of these men were powerful figures, known and respected by a lot of people in Wales.

They would only laugh at him. And, if he tried to describe the two men who had attacked him, he knew it would be almost impossible. The alley had been so dark and he had been so frightened that he had not even had time to look at them properly.

A Crack in the Dam p27, M Evans (Macmillan 'Rangers' Range 6)

8.2.2 *Speaking practice*

Speaking practice can also develop naturally out of a Reader. Writing and then practising simple dialogues from direct speech is one activity. Example 30 shows the kind of open dialogue a teacher can construct. Students talk while constructing the dialogue in pairs and can then practise asking and answering the questions.

Example 30

What do you say?

The small plane is flying low. There is a fire in the engine and the pilot has to land. He is calling for help on the radio. Imagine you are working in the control tower at a big airport. You hear the pilot and you want to help him. Write out the questions you have to ask the pilot.

CT: _____

Pilot: *I have a fire in my engine.*

CT: _____

Pilot: I can't land *because of the trees.*

CT: _____

Pilot: Wait! I see a lake. I am going to land *on the ice.*

CT: _____

Pilot: We are *on the ground near a lake.*

CT: _____

Pilot: *One of the passengers* is hurt.

CT: _____

Pilot: We need *help.*

Activity Book for *Flying Doctor* p7, Alwyn Cox
(Macmillan 'Rangers' Range 2)

8.2.3 *Writing practice*

Readers provide many opportunities to set up class work for developing writing skills. Writing about the book is useful for more advanced students: summaries, essays and reviews. Review writing was introduced in Chapter 6 as an activity to accompany individualised reading. It is also a useful class activity.

The Book Review worksheet (Figure 24) can be used for note making. When students have finished making notes, the teacher can use some sections for checking comprehension by asking students what they have written. As students report on their answers to section D, the teacher can build up lists of useful vocabulary on the blackboard, eg *exciting, tragic, amusing, sad, dramatic, serious*, to help students express their opinions. The guide (Figure 24) can then be discussed as a way of organising a review, ordering the information and opinions into a well-developed piece of writing.

A critical review can also be successfully incorporated into the content of a letter to the author. This provides an authentic context in which students practise letter writing. If the letters are collected together and sent off to the publisher, students might even get a reply from the author.

Developing writing tasks *out of* the book is another possibility. Students could follow up a topic and collect information about lost cities, space programmes, or folk tales, and write up the project in English. Writing can also take models *from* the book. A description of a place, for example, can be studied for its content and organisation of information and students can follow it to produce their own local description. A famous life story can be studied for its vocabulary, tense sequences and time adverbials and students can choose a local figure to write a biography about. Sometimes, the content of a story provides a natural context for writing. Example 31 demonstrates how letter writing can be developed out of the content of the story as students have to imagine what one character might write about her situation.

Example 31

Time to write
What do you think Alice says? Fill in the words.

Dear Mother and Father,

I am very happy in Torida. Mr and Mrs
Hall are _____ and I have no
trouble _____ .

Every day we _____ and Mrs Hall
paints while _____ .
After Lunch _____ then I give _____
_____ from _____ .
In the evening _____ . Sometimes _____
_____ with Mr and Mrs Hall.

With love from

Alice

Activity Book for *Held to Ransom* p10,
Sylvia Moody (Macmillan 'Rangers' Range 3)

8.2.4 *Integrated skills work*

Finally, teachers can develop integrated skills work out of reading. For example, students can be asked to devise an interview with a character in the book. The steps for this activity can be as follows:

1 The teacher suggests a character from the book who is going to be 'interviewed' and asks students what they would like to find out about him or her.
2 Students write down a few questions individually in their notebooks.
3 The teacher elicits questions from the class and writes them on the blackboard, correcting structures etc. Students copy the questions into their books.
4 Students work in pairs to find answers to the questions in the Reader or to make up imaginary answers.
5 Teacher checks answers with the class.
6 Students work out a dialogue in pairs, writing down questions and answers to create an 'interview'. Teacher monitors and helps.
7 Some pairs of students read out their interviews to the class.

In this way students develop their skills of reading, writing and speaking, and are motivated by the variety of activity in the lesson.

The range of examples in this chapter will hopefully serve as a source of ideas for activities and exercises which teachers can devise for more intensive language work in their own classrooms.

Conclusion

This book has set out to say five basic things about using graded Readers. Here they are in summary form.

- That care and sensitivity is needed in the selection of Readers and that teachers need a checklist of criteria to go through so that books can be chosen to suit the learners.

- That forms of classroom management, organisation of book resources, and grouping of students should be appropriate to local conditions, to what the pupils can respond to and to what the teacher feels confident with. The ideal method is that of borrowing books from a class library for individualised reading, but, to be effective this approach requires careful training of students and great sensitivity from teachers.

- That methods of reading and ways of approaching reading should relate to good language learning practice within the particular educational context.

- That it is valuable to experiment with different kinds of work in relation to graded Readers but the work may not necessarily just be after the reading (it can be before or while reading) and such work is not always absolutely necessary. The main goal is fluent, direct and pleasurable reading.

- That the best kind of learning is self directed learning and extensive reading provides opportunities for students to develop independence from the teacher and, ultimately, from graded Readers themselves as they move through careful stages to authentic reading material.

Appendix I
Readers for Africa

There are many sets of Readers produced for specific teaching contexts. Here, for example are some Readers produced especially for Africa.

East African Publishing House
East Africa Junior Library
East Africa Readers Library
East Africa Senior Library
Safari Adventure Books

Oxford University Press
Oxford Primary Stories for Nigeria

Macmillan Publishers Ltd
Controlled Readers for Africa
Pacesetters

Macmillan Nigeria Publishers Ltd
Winners

Thomas Nelson and Sons Ltd
Young Childrens' Readers for Africa
New Nation English Storybooks

George Harrap
African Library

Evans Brothers Ltd
Plays for African Schools
English Readers

Appendix II
Publishers' handbooks

The following handbooks published by the major producers of graded Readers are a useful source of information about criteria for grading and often contain ideas for exploitation of Readers in the classroom:

A Guide to Collins English Library
Evans Graded Reading Teachers' Guide
Longman Structural Readers Handbook
Longman Graded Reading Index
Macmillan Guide to Rangers
Heinemann Guided Readers Handbook

Longman has also produced a useful guide and ideas book: *How to Make the Most of Graded Readers on Cassette* (Ed) Janet Tadman

Appendix III
The Malaysian reading scheme

An interesting project in the use of graded Readers was launched in Malaysia in 1976 when the English Language Reading Programme (ELRP) was set up in 19 residential schools. By 1983 the number of schools involved had risen to over 200. The aim of the programme was primarily to increase students' exposure to English both inside and outside the classroom and thereby to increase their speed of learning English.

To achieve this aim, the reading programme involved two complementary components: Library Boxes and Class Readers. Both components were introduced into the residential schools from the start, but only the Library Boxes have so far been introduced into the day schools.

Each class has a Library Box of about 50 graded Readers from which a student can borrow at least one title a week to read at home or in 'odd' moments between lessons. The school is provided with advice on running the scheme and with entry tests to ascertain reading levels. The Readers arrive at the school as a complete package with ready-classified boxes and accession lists, questions for each title and self-correcting answer cards.

Schools which can afford class Readers as well (one copy of the same title per student) give every class two or three titles per term. A Teaching File accompanies each class Reader and this sets out a teaching programme for one lesson a week for four weeks. The file contains notes on the background of the book, comprehension tests and details of activities that can exploit the text and help to motivate the student.

The Library Box Readers are designed to give extensive practice in direct, fluent reading at a level at which students have little difficulty with the language. Where economic necessity limits a school to only one component, Library Boxes are chosen first because they provide maximum exposure to English.

The level of the Class Readers, on the other hand, is always a little higher than the Library Readers because the teacher can help students understand the text. Thus, the Class Reader, for use in supported learning, can stretch the students' comprehension and language competence.

The reading scheme has proved to be a very effective learning resource. Commercially-available simplified Readers are classified into seven levels (G-A) for pupils following the Lower Secondary School Syllabus and a range of unsimplified Readers are divided into three levels (X,Y,Z,) for the Upper Secondary School Syllabus. Provision is also made for the small number of students who can already read unsimplified books when they enter secondary school.

It is interesting to see the decisions taken about levels. The Lower Secondary Syllabus requires students to read to a level of 2,200 words by the end of Form III. Other criteria used to determine choice are many of those discussed in Chapter 3: complexity of structures, amount and type of illustrations, clarity of the story and cost. The headword levels may interest teachers involved in setting up similar programmes in schools.

level	approximate word count	level	approximate word count
G	300+	C	1,400+
F	500+	B	1,800+
E	500+	A	2,000+
D	1,100+		

Individualised reading with library books is checked in two ways.
1 Firstly through a reading chart (this general idea is discussed in

5.2) which can be pinned to the wall. This lists the titles of Readers along the top and students' names on the left hand side. Students make entries whenever they finish books, marking the chart with a letter to denote their degree of enjoyment and a number to show how difficult they found it to read.

Enjoyment	Easy/Difficult
A = enjoyed the book very much	1 = rather easy
B = quite enjoyed the book	2 = about right
C = didn't enjoy the book	3 = rather difficult
D = didn't finish the book	

2 Secondly, each student keeps a reading notebook in which he answers questions pasted in the back of each Reader. These can be checked by the student himself by reference to a self correcting card which comes with the package.

Putting the ELRP into practice was complicated initially by large mixed ability classes and it became necessary to 'set' classes, through a diagnostic cloze test (see 3.3.4 for a discussion of cloze tests) in the first term of secondary school. Now well-established practice, this allows a class to be divided into sets of a more homogeneous level for entry to the reading programme.

In 1983 a study was made of the ELRP in view of the Ministry of Education's wish to extend the scheme to all secondary schools. David Hill, of the Edinburgh Project on Extensive Reading (Institute for Applied Language Studies, University of Edinburgh) evaluated the Library Box programme in particular and recommended a number of modifications, but it is encouraging for teachers who wish to develop the use of graded Readers in their own institutions to note his comment

'. . . teachers speak of a greater interest in English lessons, a greater interest in books and greater general knowledge. They are confident that extensive reading assists acquisition of new language items and reinforces mastery of those already learned.'

Bibliography and further reading

Abbot, G and Wingard P (Eds) (1981) *The Teaching of English as an International Language: A Practical Guide* Collins, London

Allen, J P B and Widdowson H G (1978) 'Teaching the Communicative Use of English' in Mackay, R and Mountford, A *English for Specific Purposes* Longman, London

Anderson, J 'Selecting a Suitable Reader: procedures for teachers to assess language difficulty' in *Regional English Language Centre Journal* Vol 2 No 2 1971

Bright, J A and McGregor G P (1970, tenth impression 1979) *Teaching English as a Second Language* Longman, London

Brumfit, C J (1979) *Readers for Foreign Learners of English* ETIC Information Guide No 7, The British Council.

Calthrop, K (1971) *Reading Together — an investigation into the Use of the Class Reader* Heinemann Educational, London

Davies, E and Whitney, N (1979) Reasons for Reading: Teachers' Guide Heinemann Educational Books, London

Davies, A and Widdowson, H G 'Reading and Writing' Chapter 6 in Volume 3 of *The Edinburgh Course in Applied Linguistics* (Eds Allen, J P B and S Pit Corder) OUP (1974)

De Melker, R 'Guiding Extensive Novel Reading through Questions' pps 63-67 in *Selections from Modern English Teacher* (Ed Moorwood, Helen) Longman, London (1978)

Goodman, K S 'Reading: A Psycholinguistic Guessing Game' (1968) in *Journal of the Reading Specialist* 6 pps 126-135

Halliday, M A K and Hasan, Ruqaiya (1976) *Cohesion in English* Longman, London

Harrison, Colin *Readability in the Classroom* (1980) Press Syndicate of the University of Cambridge, Cambridge

Haycraft, J (1981) *An Introduction to English Language Teaching* Longman, London

Henner-Stanchina, C and Riley, P (1978) 'Aspects of Autonomous Learning' in *Individualisation in Language Learning* ELT Documents 103, The British Council.

Hill, L A and Dobbyn, M (1979) *A Teacher Training Course* Cassell EFL, London

Hindmarsh, R *Cambridge English Lexicon* (1981) Cambridge University Press, Cambridge.

Holbrook, D (1961) *English for Maturity* Cambridge University Press

Hornby, A S (1967) 'Vocabulary Control, History and Principles' in *English Language Teaching Journal* Vol 8 No 1

Lunzer, E A and Gardner W K (Eds) (1979) *The Effective Use of Reading,* Schools Council Project Report, London, Heinemann.

Mackay, R, Barkman, B and Jordan, R R (Eds) (1979) *Reading in a Second Language: Hypotheses, Organisation and Practice* Newbury House Publishers, Massachussetts

Moody, H L B (1971) *The Teaching of Literature* Longman, London

Munby, J (1979) 'Teaching Intensive Reading Skills' in Mackay, Barkman and Jordan *Reading in a Second Language* Newbury House

Nuttall, C (1982) *Teaching Reading Skills in a Foreign Language* Practical Language Teaching Series, Heinemann Educational, London

Pugh, A K (1978) *Silent Reading: an introduction to its study and teaching* Heinemann Educational, London

Rees, Alun, L W (1980) 'Reading Aloud: Suggestions for Classroom Procedure' in *English Language Teaching Journal* Vol XXXIV No 2 January 1980 pps 112-120

Rivers, W and Mary S Temperley (1978) *A Practical Guide to the Teaching of English as a Second or Foreign Language* Oxford University Press, New York

Schaefer, K 'Reading Novels with Advanced Students' in *Selections from Modern English Teacher* (Ed Moorwood, H) pps 62-63 Longman, London

Tadman, J (Ed) (1980) *How to make the Most of Graded Readers on Cassette*, Longman, Harlow

Thorndike, E L and Lorge, I (1944) *The Teacher's Wordbook of 30,000 Words*. Teachers' College, Columbia, New York

West, M (1936) *Interim Report of the Committee on Vocabulary Selection*, Carnegie

West, M (1950) 'Simplified and Abridged' *English Language Teaching Journal*, Vol V No 2 1950

West, M (1953) *A General Service List of English Words* Longman, London

West, M (1964) 'Criteria in the Selection of Simplified Reading Books' *English Language Teaching Journal* XVIII No 4.

Widdowson, H G (1975) *Stylistics and the Teaching of Literature* Longman, London

Widdowson, H G (1979, second impression 1980) *Explorations in Applied Linguistics* p164 Oxford University Press, Oxford

Widdowson, H G (1978) *Teaching Language as Communication* Oxford University Press, Oxford

Wilkins, D A (1972) *Linguistics in Language Teaching* Edward Arnold, London

Williams, E (1984) *Reading in the Language Classroom Essential Language Teaching Series* (Ed Flavell, R) Macmillan, London

Yorke, M (1980) 'Encountering the Novel: Problems and a Possible Solution' *English Language Teaching Journal* Vol XXXIV No 4 July 1980 pps 315-15

Index

activities, to promote reading 92-93
  to prepare for reading 96-99
  post-reading 95, 101-108
autonomous learning 77
background knowledge, general 44-45
  subject specific 45-46
  cultural 46-48
book diaries 101
book reviews 102-104
borrowing system 85-88
card index 86-87
cassettes, use of 92, 111-114, 116-118
catalogue, library 86-87
class library 83-93
  Readers 109-119
classification, of Readers 85
cloze procedure 53-56
complexity, of sentences 10
connectives 25-26
contextual, clues to meaning 23, 32
control, lexical 2-9, 18-19
  structural 9-14, 20
  information 14-15, 17
diaries 101
dictionaries 68-71
design, of Readers 56-59
  of a programme 116-118
extensive reading 31-34, 63-82
front covers 57
grading, general linguistic 1-2
  lexical 2-9
  structural 9-14
graphics 58-59
General Service List 3
group activities 110, 113-116
illustrations 7, 57, 110
individualised reading 76-78, 82, 94-108
information control 14-15, 17-18

intensive reading 31-34, 68, 70
interest questionnaires 63-67
interviews 95
language: use 26-31
  knowledge 22-26
  functions 28-31
length of sentences 2
lesson planning 116-118
lexical control 2-9, 18
library, book 86
  catalogue 86-87
  corner 84
linguistic grading 1-2
listening 100, 112-114, 133-135
literature 20-21, 39-41, 91-92
magazines 42-43
methods of reading 112-116
motivation 35-36, 38-41, 50
oral reading 114-116
pictures 7, 57, 110
preparation for reading 96-99
previewing 72-75
programme for reading 116-118
promoting reading 92-93
publishers, grading schemes 3-14, 49
  handbooks 49, 142
questions, types of 118-119
questionnaires, interest 63-67
readability 9-14
Readers, class 109-119
  classification of 85
  for British schools 42
  for special groups 48
  illustrations in 7, 57, 110
  promotion of 92-93
  selection of 37-61
  types of 41-44
reading, attitudes 34-36

class 109-119
  extensive/intensive 31-34, 63, 68, 70
  individualised 76-78, 82, 94-108
  preparation 96-99
  questionnaires 63-67
  records 87-90, 101
  silent 76-78
  strategies 31-34
  supported/unsupported 51-55
record keeping 87-90, 101
reference system, in texts 13
selection, of Readers 37-61
sentence, complexity 10
  length 9
silent reading 76-78

simplification 16-21
socio-cultural meaning 46-48
speaking practice, related to reading 135, 139
structural, control 9-14, 20
  exercises 127-131
technical presentation, of Readers 56-59
topic work 106, 137
typeface 58
unsupported reading 51-55
vocabulary, books 71-72
  control 2-9, 18-19
  exercises 121-127
word frequency counts 2
workcards 96-99, 106-108
writing activities 101-106, 137

Acknowledgements

The author and publishers wish to thank the following who have kindly given permission for the use of copyright material:

Edward Arnold (Publishers) Ltd for an extract from *Linguistics in Language Teaching* by D A Wilkins. Cambridge University Press for an extract from *Readability in the Classroom* by Colin Harrison, and from *English for Maturity* by David Holbrook. Chatto and Windus Ltd and Mrs Laura Huxley for an extract from *Brave New World* by Aldous Huxley. Collins Publishers for extracts from *Guide to Collins English Library*, edited by K R Cripwell and Lewis Jones and from *Crocodile* by K R Cripwell (Collins English Library, Level 1). Curtis Brown Ltd on behalf of the Estate of John Steinbeck for an extract from *The Moon is Down*. Heinemann Educational Books for extracts from *Heinemann Guided Readers Handbook* by John Milne, and *The Sky's the Limit* by Norman Whitney. David Higham Associates Ltd on behalf of John Christopher for an extract from *The White Mountain*, published by Longman Group Ltd. Longman Group Ltd for extracts from *An Introduction to English Language Teaching* by J Haycraft; from the *Handbook to Longman Structural Readers*; from 'Have You Got Your Ticket?' by Ian Serralier (Longman Structural Readers, Stage 2) and from *Mogul* by John Elliot (Longman Structural Readers, Stage 5). Oxford University Press for extracts from 'Simplified and Abridged' by Michael West in *English Language Teaching Journal* Vol. 5, No. 2,1950; from 'Reading and Writing' by A Davies and H G Widdowson in *The Edinburgh Course in Applied Linguistics* Vol. 3 1974, and from 'Reading Aloud: Suggestions for Classroom Procedure' by Alun L W Rees in *English Language Teaching Journal* Vol XXIV, No.

2, 1980. Oxford University Press Inc for extracts from *A Practical Guide to the Teaching of English as a Second or Foreign Language* by W Rivers and M S Temperley. Norman Whitney for extracts from his classroom workcards.

Every effort has been made to trace all the copyright holders but if any have been inadvertently overlooked the publishers will be pleased to make the necessary arrangement at the first opportunity.